NOTES

including
- *Introduction to the Romantic Period*
- *Life of the Poets*
- *Summaries and Commentaries*
- *Questions and Essay Topics*
- *Selected Bibliography*

by
Dougald B. MacEachen, Ph.D.
Department of English
John Carroll University

LINCOLN, NEBRASKA 68501

Editor

Gary Carey, M.A.
University of Colorado

Consulting Editor

James L. Roberts, Ph.D.
Department of English
University of Nebraska

ISBN 0-8220-0702-9
© Copyright 1971
by
C. K. Hillegass
All Rights Reserved
Printed in U.S.A.

1991 Printing

The Cliffs Notes logo, the names "Cliffs" and "Cliffs Notes," and the black and yellow diagonal-stripe cover design are all registered trademarks belonging to Cliffs Notes, Inc., and may not be used in whole or in part without written permission.

Cliffs Notes, Inc.   Lincoln, Nebraska

CONTENTS

Introduction to the Romantic Period 5

Keats Notes

Life of Keats 8

Summaries and Commentaries

    "On First Looking into Chapman's Homer" 12
    "When I Have Fears" 15
    The Eve of St. Agnes 17
    "La Belle Dame sans Merci" 21
    "Ode to Psyche" 23
    "Ode to a Grecian Urn" 26
    "Ode on Melancholy" 29
    "Ode to a Nightingale" 32
    Lamia 35
    "To Autumn" 39

Selected Bibliography 41

Shelley Notes

Life of Shelley 43

Summaries and Commentaries

    "Hymn to Intellectual Beauty" 48
    "Ozymandias" 51
    "Stanzas Written in Dejection, near Naples" 53
    "Sonnet: England in 1819" 55
    "Ode to the West Wind" 57
    "The Cloud" 60

"To a Skylark" 63
"To Night" 66
Adonais 68

Selected Bibliography 74

Introduction to the Romantic Period

The romantic period is a term applied to the literature of approximately the first third of the nineteenth century. During this time, literature began to move in channels that were not entirely new but were in strong contrast to the standard literary practice of the eighteenth century.

How the word *romantic* came to be applied to this period is something of a puzzle. Originally the word was applied to the Latin or Roman dialects used in the Roman provinces, especially France, and to the stories written in these dialects. *Romantic* is a derivative of *romant*, which was borrowed from the French *romaunt* in the sixteenth century. At first it meant only "like the old romances" but gradually it began to carry a certain taint. *Romantic*, according to L. P. Smith in his *Words and Idioms*, connoted "false and fictitious beings and feelings, without real existence in fact or in human nature"; it also suggested "old castles, mountains and forests, pastoral plains, waste and solitary places" and a "love for wild nature, for mountains and moors."

The word passed from England to France and Germany late in the seventeenth century and became a critical term for certain poets who scorned and rejected the models of the past; they prided themselves on their freedom from eighteenth-century poetic codes. In Germany, especially, the word was used in strong opposition to the term *classical*.

The grouping together of the so-called Lake poets (Wordsworth, Coleridge, and Southey) with Scott, Byron, Keats, and Shelley as the romantic poets is late Victorian, apparently as late as the middle 1880s. And it should be noted that these poets did not recognize themselves as "romantic," although they were familiar with the word and recognized that their practice differed from that of the eighteenth century. According to René Wellek in his essay "The Concept of Romanticism" *(Comparative*

Literature, Volume I), the widespread application of the word *romantic* to these writers was probably owing to Alois Brandl's *Coleridge und die romantische Schule in England (Coleridge and the Romantic School in England,* translated into English in 1887) and to Walter Pater's essay "Romanticism" in his *Appreciations* in 1889.

The reaction to the standard literary practice and critical norms of the eighteenth century occurred in many areas and in varying degrees. Reason no longer held the high place it had held in the eighteenth century; its place was taken by imagination, emotion, and individual sensibility. The eccentric and the singular took the place of the accepted conventions of the age. A concentration on the individual and the minute replaced the eighteenth-century insistence on the universal and the general. Individualism replaced objective subject matter; probably at no other time has the writer used himself as the subject of his literary works to such an extent as during the romantic period. Writers tended to regard themselves as the most interesting subject for literary creation; interest in urban life was replaced by an interest in nature, particularly in untamed nature and in solitude. Classical literature quickly lost the esteem which poets like Pope had given it. The romantic writers turned back to their own native traditions. The Medieval and Renaissance periods were ransacked for new subject matter and for literary genres that had fallen into disuse. The standard eighteenth-century heroic couplet was replaced by a variety of forms such as the ballad, the metrical romance, the sonnet, ottava rima, blank verse, and the Spenserian stanza, all of which were forms that had been neglected since Renaissance times. The romantic writers responded strongly to the impact of new forces, particularly the French Revolution and its promise of liberty, equality, and fraternity. The humanitarianism that had been developing during the eighteenth century was taken up enthusiastically by the romantic writers. Wordsworth, the great champion of the spiritual and moral values of physical nature, tried to show the natural dignity, goodness, and the worth of the common man. The combination of new interests, new attitudes, and fresh forms produced a body of literature that was strikingly different from the literature of the eighteenth century, but that is not to say that the eighteenth century had no influence on the romantic movement. Practically all of the seeds of the new literary crop had been sown in the preceding century.

The romantic period includes the work of two generations of writers. The first generation was born during the thirty and twenty years preceding 1800; the second generation was born in the last decade of the 1800s. The chief writers of the first generation were Wordsworth, Coleridge, Scott, Southey, Blake, Lamb, and Hazlitt. The essayist Thomas De Quincey, born in 1785, falls between the two generations.

Keats and Shelley belong to the second generation, along with Byron, who was older than they were by a few years. All three were influenced by the work of the writers of the first generation and, ironically, the careers of all three were cut short by death so that the writers of the first generation were still on the literary scene after the writers of the second generation had disappeared. The major writers of the second romantic generation were primarily poets; they produced little prose, outside of their letters. Another striking difference between the two generations is that the writers of the first generation, with the exception of Blake, all gained literary reputations during their lifetime. Of the writers of the second generation, only Byron enjoyed fame while he was alive, more fame than any of the other romantic writers, with perhaps the exception of Scott, but Keats and Shelley had relatively few readers while they were alive. It was not until the Victorian era that Keats and Shelley became recognized as major romantic poets.

Keats Notes

LIFE OF KEATS

John Keats was born on October 31, 1795, on the northern outskirts of London. His father was Thomas Keats, manager of the Swan and Hoop, a livery stable, and his mother was Frances Jennings, the daughter of the proprietor of the stables. In 1803, Keats entered John Clarke's school in Enfield, about ten miles from London. Clarke was a liberal and his influence may have contributed to Keats' political development. The school, surprisingly, had a wider curriculum than such prestigious public schools as Eton. There were about seventy-five boys in attendance. Its rural location may have fostered Keats' love of nature. John was popular with the other boys and won a reputation as an able fighter, in spite of his small size, but was not outstanding as a scholar.

On April 15, 1804, John's father was thrown from a horse and died from a skull fracture. His mother then married a bank clerk whom she soon left. Her second husband sold the stables and the four Keats children were left without a home.

In March, 1805, John's grandfather died, leaving the children without a male protector. The mother seems to have dropped out of their lives, and so their grandmother, Mrs. Jennings, took them into her house. Their mother reappeared in 1808, but died of tuberculosis in 1810. After his mother's death, Keats developed a love of reading, including the thrillers popular in his time. In his last two or three terms at Enfield he won several prizes and even began a prose translation of Virgil's *Aeneid*. At this time he made a friend of Cowden Clarke, eight years his senior, who had been his tutor in his first years at Enfield. Clarke was instrumental in fostering a love of music and poetry in Keats.

Possibly because he had watched his mother die, Keats decided to become a doctor and, in 1811, when he reached the age of sixteen, he was apprenticed to a Dr. Hammond. Not until he was eighteen did he become deeply interested in poetry. It was apparently Cowden Clarke's lending Keats a copy of Spenser's *Faerie Queene* that furnished the stimulus. His first poem was an imitation of Spenser. Keats has often been compared to Spenser in his richness of description.

In 1815, Keats ended his apprenticeship with Dr. Hammond and matriculated at Guy's Hospital for one term (six months). In the beginning, Keats was an industrious student, but in the spring of 1816 he seems to have begun to lose his interest in medicine in favor of poetry. However, he passed his examinations in July, 1816, and was qualified to practice as an apothecary and a surgeon.

At this time Keats renewed his friendship with Clarke, met another young poet, John Hamilton Reynolds, and was introduced to the essayist, journalist, and poet Leigh Hunt, who was impressed by the poetry Keats had written so far. His friendship with Hunt was to have an important effect on his life. Hunt deepened his interest in poetry and made him a liberal in politics. His association with Hunt, however, who was a well-known liberal, brought upon him the hostility of the influential Tory critics.

Early in 1817, Keats gave up medicine for poetry. His career at Guy's Hospital had been a successful one, but his fascination with poetry was stronger, and he had proved, at least to his own satisfaction, that he could write poetry. His modest inheritance would support him, he thought, until he had made his way in poetry. His first volume, published by Shelley's publisher, Ollier, appeared March 3, 1817. It was a mediocre achievement, but it contained "Chapman's Homer." An acute critic should have been able to see, at least on the basis of this one poem, that the author showed promise, but unfortunately no acute and influential critic appeared as Keats' champion. The volume went almost unnoticed. The many new friends he had made since coming to London—Keats had a gift for friendship—were hopeful, but there was little they could do.

Keats now decided to try his hand at a long poem. The result was *Endymion,* an involved romance in the Elizabethan style, in which a mortal, the shepherd Endymion, was wedded to the goddess Diana and won immortal bliss. Keats worked on it from April to November, 1817, and it appeared in April, 1818. Before the year was over, *Endymion* was harshly reviewed in *Blackwood's Magazine* and the *Quarterly Review.* These reviews effectively stopped the sales of the volume. *Endymion,* it must be said, while containing many good lines and passages, is not a good poem, but worse poems now forgotten have won fame and financial rewards for their authors. If *Endymion* had been written by a respected Tory poet, it might have been hailed as a fine poem by *Blackwood's* and the *Quarterly.* Keats' politics happened to be the wrong ones in 1818.

An important change in Keats' life was a walking tour that he took through the Lake Country, up into Scotland, and a short trip to Ireland, with one of his friends, Charles Brown, in the summer of 1818. The trip lasted from June to August and reached its terminus in Cromarty, Scotland. The walking tour broadened Keats' acquaintance with his environment and with varieties of people. The hardships which Keats and Brown had to endure, often spending the night on the mud floor of a shepherd's hut, may have weakened Keats' constitution and shortened his life. In Inverness, he developed a sore throat and decided to return to London by boat. The trip itself produced very little poetry.

In September, Keats began a new long poem, *Hyperion,* which he never finished. The blank verse of *Hyperion* revealed that Keats had become a first-class poet. His firm control of language in *Hyperion* is truly astonishing. *Endymion* and *Hyperion* could have been the work of two different poets.

During the last months of 1818, Keats nursed his brother Tom, who had been stricken with tuberculosis. Tom died on December 1 at the age of nineteen. The three months which Keats spent nursing his brother exposed the already weakened poet to tuberculosis, and, by the spring of 1819, he showed many of the symptoms of the disease—depression, hoarseness, insomnia, and an ulcerated sore throat.

In April and May of 1819, Keats experienced a burst of energy and wrote "Ode to Psyche," "Ode on Melancholy," "Ode on a Grecian Urn," and "Ode on Indolence." In January he wrote his most perfect narrative poem, *The Eve of St. Agnes*.

Keats' future was now a problem. He was running out of money—and was in love with a lively and lovely girl, Fanny Brawne. He thought of becoming a ship's surgeon. His friend Brown, who had written a successful play, suggested that they write a tragedy together that might be a financial success. As Keats needed solitude for a lengthy work, on June 27 he left for the Isle of Wight, where he had begun *Endymion*. Brown joined him there and supplied the plot while Keats supplied the words. They spent the summer of 1819 working on *Otho the Great*. During this summer, Keats also wrote his lengthy narrative poem *Lamia*, which he hoped would prove popular. Unfortunately, neither of the legitimate theaters, Drury Lane and Covent Garden, would take a chance on *Otho*, which was a decidely mediocre work, but not worse than some other plays staged by these two theaters.

After this summer, Keats accomplished very little. He worked at *Hyperion* now and then, began a new play (*King Stephen*), began a satire, and wrote his superb "To Autumn." He had very little money left and he was filled with anxieties, but nevertheless he and Fanny Brawne became secretly engaged. In February, 1820, Keats had a hemorrhage in his lungs; he began to cough blood and soon became an invalid.

Keats' third and last volume of poetry came out July 1, 1820, when he was staying with the Hunts and recovering from another hemorrhage. Gradually the volume began to receive favorable reviews, including one in the influential *Edinburgh Review*. Nevertheless the volume sold slowly. Keats did not begin to receive attention as a poet until after the romantic period was over.

On the advice of two doctors, Keats decided to go to Italy, a trip that was often a last resort when one was stricken with tuberculosis. John Taylor, who had published Keats' last volume, put up the money for the Italian trip. The expected sales of the *Lamia* volume were the security for the loan.

Keats sailed from London on September 17, 1821, and arrived in Naples almost a month later. From there, he travelled to Rome, where he rented an apartment overlooking the famous "Spanish Steps." There, attended by his painter friend Joseph Severn, he entered the last stages of tuberculosis and died on February 23, 1821. He was buried in the Protestant Cemetery in Rome near the stately Pyramid of Caius Cestius. On his tombstone appears, at his own request, the words "Here lies one whose name was writ in water." The thousands of visitors who read these words every year are eloquent proof of how greatly he underestimated his poetic achievement.

SUMMARIES AND COMMENTARIES

"On First Looking into Chapman's Homer"

Summary

Keats has wide experience in the reading of poetry and is familiar with Homer's *Iliad* and *Odyssey*, but not until now has he had the special aesthetic enjoyment to be gained from reading Homer in the translation of George Chapman. For him, the discovery of Homer as translated by Chapman provides the same kind of overwhelming excitement felt by an astronomer who has discovered a new planet or by Cortez when he first saw the Pacific from a summit in Central America.

Commentary

Keats composed his most famous sonnet when he was only twenty years old and had comparatively little experience in the writing of sonnets. The poem is brilliant testimony of the effect of poetry on Keats. He had spent a night in the autumn of 1816 reading poetry with his friend Charles Cowden Clarke, who introduced him to some of the best passages in George Chapman's translation of Homer. Keats was delighted with the vigorous language of the Elizabethan; to him, Chapman spoke out "loud and bold." After Keats left Clarke, around daybreak, he walked to his lodgings, sat down at his desk, wrote his tribute to Chapman, and had a copy of it on his friend's breakfast table by ten o'clock in the morning. The poem seems to have been composed in the white heat of excitement, in a flash of inspiration. Keats made very few changes in it, but the changes he made show that he realized that inspiration is not enough; it must be followed by critical judgment. Keats' changes in the poem are all improvements.

It is appropriate that the finest poem in Keats' first volume of poetry should be about poetry. At the time, poetry meant more to him than anything else in the world. He was on the point of giving up the security of a career in medicine for the uncertainties of a career in poetry. The first four lines of "Chapman's Homer" are a statement of the experience he has already had as a reader of poetry: "Much have I travell'd in the realms of gold. . . ." In poetry he has found the gold that Cortez, and the other conquistadors he had read about in William Robertson's *History of America,* had searched for so feverishly. As Keats is still young, there are innumerable discoveries of "realms of gold" awaiting him. In "Chapman's Homer," he excitedly reports one such discovery.

To convey to the reader the thrill of discovery he has experienced in hearing his friend Clarke read from Chapman's Homer to him, he uses two similes that are both beautiful and apt. "Then felt I like some watcher of the skies/ When a new planet swims into his ken." The discovery of a new planet is so rare that only one had been made between ancient times and 1781, when Sir William Herschel discovered the planet Uranus. Keats, of course, may not have had Herschel in mind, but it was the rarity of such a discovery and the emotions which would overwhelm the discoverer that counted. Nothing less would give the reader an adequate idea of what happened to Keats when he "heard Chapman speak out loud and bold." "Swims," the verb used to describe the way in which a heavenly body would move into the circular lens of an astronomer's telescope, suggests perfectly the motion of a planet as seen from the earth.

The second simile used by Keats is unquestionably the most impressive part of the sonnet. It is made up of a number of details that fit together into an artistically pleasing whole. Cortez is "stout," that is, fearless, and he is alert, "with eagle eyes." Only men such as he discover Pacific Oceans. His men stand about him in silent awe, looking "at each other with a wild surmise." Their imaginations are flooded by a bewildering variety of guesses as to what lies beyond the horizon, new Americas perhaps, filled with gold and fabulous jewels and untold possibilities of further discoveries. They are so choked with emotion that they cannot speak. This is one of the great moments of history, and Keats boldly appropriates it to express his own feelings of having made a thrilling discovery beyond which there may lie countless other similar discoveries as he increases his acquaintance with the world of poetry.

The two similes that swam "into his ken" as the poem formed itself in his mind are in keeping with the language of travel and discovery that he uses in the octave of his sonnet. They give it a unity of imagery that makes of the whole a tightly knit statement of what was for Keats, ardent lover of poetry that he was, a profoundly felt experience.

A Petrarchan sonnet must not only be unified, like any other poem, but the thought must also make a change of direction, or "turn," at the beginning of the sestet. Keats' turn is his two comparisons taken from astronomy and exploration. Unity and coherence are assured not only by carrying the idea of discovery all the way through the poem, but also by using the linking words "Much" and "Oft" to begin the two halves of his octave and the word "Then" to begin his sestet. Keats, in spite of his limited experience in sonnet writing before "Chapman's Homer," composed what is probably one of the finest Petrarchan sonnets in English poetry.

In his excitement, Keats substituted the name of Cortez for Balboa in his sonnet. In his school days he had read about Cortez' conquest of Mexico and Balboa's discovery of the Pacific Ocean on an expedition in Darien, an old name for part of Central America, in William Robertson's *History of America*. In search of a historical example of an exciting discovery, Keats put Cortez where historically Cortez never was and made him seem to be the discoverer of the Pacific Ocean. It is not known whether Keats or any of his friends ever became aware of the error. It is a slight blemish in a fine poem, but, as many critics have pointed out, in poetry one looks for truth in human nature rather than for historical truth. Ideally, both should go together.

Questions and Essay Topics

1. Read a few pages of Chapman's Homer and try to ascertain why Keats found it so exciting.

2. Look up definitions of the Petrarchan and the Shakespearean sonnet. What are the forms of each?

3. What does Keats mean by "pure serene"?

4. Look up Apollo in any standard manual of mythology. What is associated with Apollo?

"When I Have Fears"

Summary

When Keats experiences feelings of fear (1) that he may die before he has written the volumes of poetry that he is convinced he is capable of writing, (2) that he may never write a long metrical romance, fragments of which float through his mind, and (3) that he may never again see a certain woman and so never experience the raptures of passionate love—then he feels that he is alone in the world and that love and fame are worthless.

Commentary

In "When I Have Fears," Keats turns to the Shakespearean sonnet with its abab, cdcd, efef, gg rhyme scheme and its division into three quatrains and a concluding couplet. It was written after Keats made a close study of Shakespeare's songs and sonnets and, in its development, it imitates closely one of Shakespeare's own sonnet patterns. The three quatrains are subordinate clauses dependent on the word "when"; the concluding couplet is introduced by the word "then." The sonnet, like "On First Looking into Chapman's Homer," is constructed with care. Like "Chapman's Homer," it is concerned with the subject of poetry, to which Keats adds another favorite theme, that of love.

The sonnet is distinguished by Keats' characteristic melodiousness and by his very distinctive style, which is marked by the presence of archaic words borrowed from the Elizabethan poets. The first line, "When I have fears that I may cease to be," appeals at once to the ear and is a compelling invitation to the reader to go on with the poem. "Before high-piled books, in charact'ry,/ Hold like rich garners the full-ripen'd grain" contains two words, *charact'ry* and *garners*, that are quite remote from the kind of language recommended by Wordsworth in his famous preface to the second edition of *Lyrical Ballads* and quite remote from the language used by Keats in conversation with his friends.

"When I Have Fears" is a very personal confession of an emotion that intruded itself into the fabric of Keats' existence from at least 1816 on, the fear of an early death. The fact that both his parents were short-lived may account for the presence of this disturbing fear. In the poem, the existence of this fear annihilates both the poet's fame, which Keats ardently longed for, and the love that is so important in his poetry and in his life. As it happened, Keats was cheated by death of enjoying the fame that his poetry eventually gained for him and of marrying Fanny Brawne, the woman he loved so passionately. This fact gives the poem a pathos that helps to single it out from among the more than sixty sonnets Keats wrote.

The "fair creature of an hour" that Keats addresses in the poem was probably a beautiful woman Keats had seen in Vauxhall Gardens, an amusement park, in 1814. Keats makes her into an archetype of feminine loveliness, an embodiment of

Venus, and she remained in his memory for several years; in 1818 he addressed to her the sonnet "To a Lady Seen for a Few Moments at Vauxhall." "When I Have Fears" was written the same year. One of his earliest poems, "Fill for Me a Brimming Bowl," written in 1814, also concerns this lovely lady. In the poem, he promises that "even so for ever shall she be/ The Halo of my Memory."

Questions and Essay Topics

1. What does Keats mean by "huge cloudy symbols of a high romance"?

2. Find out what efforts have been made to identify the "fair creature of an hour" of the poem.

3. Do you think that Keats is indebted to Shakespeare for materials and attitudes, as well as for form, in "When I Have Fears"?

4. What is a garner?

The Eve of St. Agnes

Summary

The setting is a medieval castle, the time is January 20, the eve of the Feast of St. Agnes. Madeline, the daughter of the lord of the castle, is looking forward to midnight, for she has been assured by "old dames" that, if she performs certain rites, she will have a magical vision of her lover at midnight in her dreams. Madeline believes in this old superstitition and prepares to do all that is required, such as going supperless to bed.

On this same evening, Porphyro, who is in love with Madeline and whom she loves, manages to get into the castle unobserved. Madeline's family regards Porphyro as an enemy whom they are ready to kill on sight. The presence of many guests in the castle helps make it possible for Porphyro to escape notice. By chance he meets Madeline's old nurse, Angela, who is his friend; she tells him of Madeline's quaint superstition. At once the idea of making Madeline's belief become reality by his presence in her bedroom at midnight flashes into his mind. He assures Angela that he means no harm and she reluctantly agrees to help him. She leads him to Madeline's chamber where he hides in a closet.

Madeline soon enters and, her mind filled with the thought of the wonderful vision she will soon have, goes to bed and falls asleep. The ritual she has performed produces the expected result; her sleep becomes the sleep of enchantment and Porphyro, looking as if immortalized, fills her dreams.

After Madeline falls asleep, Porphyro leaves the closet and approaches her bed in order to awaken her. His whispering does not stir her; her sleep is "a midnight charm/ Impossible to melt as iced stream." He picks up her lute and plays it close to her ear. Suddenly her eyes open wide but she remains in the grip of the magic spell. Then "there was a painful change, that nigh expell'd/ The blisses of her dream so pure and deep." She now sees Porphyro, not immortal as in her dream, but in his ordinary mortality. The contrast is so great that Madeline even thinks that the human Porphyro is on the point of death. She wants her visionary Porphyro back again. Her wish is granted; the operations of magic are powerful enough to enable Porphyro, "beyond a mortal man impassion'd far," to enter her dream vision and there they are united in a mystic marriage.

When the magic visionary state comes to an end, Madeline expresses her fear that Porphyro will abandon her, "a deceived thing;—/ A dove forlorn and lost with sick unpruned wing." Porphyro, who now addresses her as his bride, urges her to leave the castle with him. "Awake! arise! my love, and fearless be,/ For o'er the southern moors I have a home for thee."

The two leave the castle undetected and go out into the storm. That night the baron and all his guests have bad dreams, and Angela and the old Beadsman both die.

Commentary

In *The Eve of St. Agnes*, Keats uses the metrical romance or narrative verse form cultivated extensively by medieval poets and revived by the romantic poets. Scott and Byron became the most popular writers of verse narrative. Keats' metrical pattern is the iambic nine-line Spenserian stanza that earlier poets had found suitable for descriptive and meditative poetry. Because of its length and slow movement, the Spenserian stanza is not well adapted to the demands of narrative verse. It inhibits rapidity of pace, and the concluding iambic hexameter line, as one critic has remarked, creates the effect of throwing out an anchor at the end of every stanza.

Keats clearly was not very interested in writing lively narrative in *The Eve of St. Agnes*. The story is trifling and the characters are of no great interest. Porphyro is an idealized knight who will face any danger whatsoever to see his lady love, and Madeline is reduced to an exquisitely lovely and loving young lady. Keats is interested in celebrating romantic love; romantic love is literally a heavenly experience, and for its culmination Keats puts his lovers temporarily in a heaven that is realized through magic. *The Eve of St. Agnes* is, in part, a poem of the supernatural which the romantic poets were so fond of employing.

The Eve of St. Agnes is a heavily descriptive poem; it is like a painting that is filled with carefully observed and minute detail. In this respect, it was a labor of love for Keats and provided him with an opportunity to exploit his innate sensuousness. Imagery such as "he follow'd through a lowly arched way,/ Brushing the cobwebs with his lofty plume," all of stanzas XXIV and XXV describing the stained glass window in Madeline's room and Madeline's appearance transformed by moonlight passing through the stained glass, stanza XXX cataloguing the foods placed on the table in Madeline's room, the lines "the arras, rich with horseman, hawk, and hound,/ Flutter'd in the besieging wind's uproar;/ And the long carpets rose along the gusty floor," show Keats' picture-making mind at work. The poem has to be read with scrupulous attention; every detail makes a distinctive contribution and even though much of what is in the poem is there for its own sake, everything at the same time makes its contribution to the exaltation of romantic love. Some critics view the poem as Keats' celebration of his first and only experience of romance. It was written not long after Keats and Fanny Brawne had fallen in love.

Readers have been struck by Keats' use of contrast in *The Eve of St. Agnes;* it is one of the chief aesthetic devices employed in the poem. The special effect of contrast is that it draws attention to all the details so that none are missed. Keats deliberately emphasizes the bitterly cold weather of St. Agnes' Eve so that ultimately the delightful warmth of happy love is emphasized. The owl, the hare, and the sheep are all affected by the cold although all three are particularly well protected by nature against it: "The owl, for all his feathers, was a-cold." The hatred of Madeline's relatives for Porphyro, for whatever reason, highlights the love of Madeline and Porphyro for each other. Age is contrasted with youth; the poverty and self-denial of the Beadsman are contrasted with the richness of the feast that Porphyro prepares for Madeline.

All the senses are appealed to at one time or another throughout the course of the poem, but, as in most poems, it is the sense of sight that is chiefly appealed to. The most striking example of Keats' appeal to the sense of sight is to be found in his description of the stained glass window in Madeline's room. This window was "diamonded with panes of quaint device,/ Innumerable of stains and splendid dyes." Madeline is transformed into a "splendid angel" by the stained glass as the moonlight shines through it:

> Full on this casement shone the wintry moon,
> And threw warm gules on Madeline's fair breast,
> As down she knelt for heaven's grace and boon;
> Rose-bloom fell on her hands, together prest,
> And on her silver cross soft amethyst,
> And on her hair a glory, like a saint:
> She seem'd a splendid angel, newly drest,
> Save wings, for heaven: — Porphyro grew faint:
> She knelt, so pure a thing, so free from mortal taint.

Keats put a stained glass window in Madeline's room in order to glorify her and put her firmly at the center of his story.

The concluding stanza of the poem raises a problem. Why does Keats have Angela, who had helped Porphyro and Madeline achieve a happy issue to their love, and the Beadsman, who had nothing to do with it, die at the end of the story? Their death does not come as a total surprise, for earlier in the poem Keats implied that both might die soon. Possibly Keats, looking beyond the end of his story, saw that Angela would be punished for not reporting the presence of Porphyro in the castle and for helping him. Death removes her from the reach of punishment. Keats may have used the death of the Beadsman, to whom he had devoted two and a half stanzas at the beginning of the poem, to close off his story. And so the Beadsman "For aye unsought for slept among his ashes cold." Keats needed a good concluding stanza to his poem, whose main characters disappear from the scene in the next to last stanza, and so the lives of his two minor characters end with the end of the poem.

Questions and Essay Topics

1. What is the role of the Beadsman in the poem? Is it an essential one?

2. Trace the imagery in the poem that appeals to the ear.

3. Why does Keats have food placed in Madeline's chamber?

"La Belle Dame sans Merci" (original version)

Summary

An unidentified speaker asks a knight what afflicts him. The knight is pale, haggard, and obviously dying. "And on thy cheeks a fading rose/ Fast withereth too—." The knight answers that he met a beautiful lady, "a faery's child" who had looked at him as if she loved him. When he set her on his horse, she led him to her cave. There she had sung him to sleep. In his sleep he had nightmarish dreams. Pale kings, princes, and warriors told him that he had been enslaved by a beautiful but cruel lady. When he awoke, the lady was gone and he was lying on a cold hillside.

Commentary

"La Belle Dame sans Merci" is a ballad, a medieval genre revived by the romantic poets. Keats uses the so-called ballad stanza, a quatrain in alternating iambic tetrameter and trimeter lines. The shortening of the fourth line in each stanza of Keats' poem makes the stanza seem a self-contained unit, gives the ballad a deliberate and slow movement, and is pleasing to the ear. Keats uses a number of the stylistic characteristics of the ballad, such as simplicity of language, repetition, and absence of details; like some of the old ballads, it deals with the supernatural. Keats' economical manner of telling a story in "La Belle Dame sans Merci" is the direct opposite of his lavish manner in *The Eve of St. Agnes*. Part of the fascination exerted by the poem comes from Keats' use of understatement.

Keats sets his simple story of love and death in a bleak wintry landscape that is appropriate to it: "The sedge has wither'd from the lake/ And no birds sing!" The repetition of these two lines, with minor variations, as the concluding lines of the poem emphasizes the fate of the unfortunate knight and neatly encloses the poem in a frame by bringing it back to its beginning.

In keeping with the ballad tradition, Keats does not identify his questioner, or the knight, or the destructively beautiful lady. What Keats does not include in his poem contributes as much to it in arousing the reader's imagination as what he puts into it. La belle dame sans merci, the beautiful lady without pity, is a *femme fatale,* a Circelike figure who attracts lovers only to destroy them by her supernatural powers. She destroys because it is her nature to destroy. Keats could have found patterns for his "faery's child" in folk mythology, classical literature, Renaissance poetry, or the medieval ballad. With a few skillful touches, he creates a woman who is at once beautiful, erotically attractive, fascinating, and deadly.

Some readers see the poem as Keats' personal rebellion against the pains of love. In his letters and in some of his poems, he reveals that he did experience the pains, as well as the pleasures, of love and that he resented the pains, particularly the loss of freedom that came with falling in love. However, the ballad is a very objective form, and it may be best to read "La Belle Dame sans Merci" as pure story and no more. How Keats felt about his love for Fanny Brawne we can discover in the several poems he addressed to her, as well as in his letters.

Questions and Essay Topics

1. Keats wrote a revised version of "La Belle Dame sans Merci." Compare the two versions and decide which is the better one.

2. What does Keats mean by "in language strange" in the poem?

3. Find some other examples of "fatal women" in English poetry.

4. Is there any hint in the poem that the food given to the knight by the "belle dame" was poisoned?

5. Look up the ballad in a handbook of literature and find out what its various characteristics are.

"Ode to Psyche"

Summary

The poet imagines that he has either seen or dreamed that he has seen the winged goddess Psyche while he was wandering in a forest. She lay in the grass in a grotto made of leaves and flowers in the embrace of Adonis.

He addresses her as the "latest born and loveliest vision far/ Of all Olympus' faded hierarchy!" Although she is fairer than all other goddesses, there is no temple to her with an altar and a choir of virgins to sing hymns to her. No one plays a musical instrument in her honor nor offers incense to her. No shrine or grove is sacred to her. No oracle or priest serves her. Keats therefore will be her choir, her lute, her incense, her shrine, her grove, her oracle, and her prophet. He will be her priest and build a temple in his mind to her. Thoughts will serve for pine trees and among them will be her sanctuary which his imagination will decorate with flowers of every variety. In her sanctuary there will be a "bright torch" and a window open at night through which her lover, Cupid, may enter.

Commentary

"Ode to Psyche" is the first of a group of odes which Keats composed in April and May, 1819. It is one of Keats' best and most significant poems, but it has not gained the interest of readers in the way that his famous "Ode on a Grecian Urn" or "Ode to a Nightingale" have. It does not measure up to them in power of language, beauty of form, or interest of theme.

The goddess Psyche does not belong in the pantheon of classical mythology. She is the creation of Apuleius, the second century A.D. Latin author of *The Golden Ass*. In this novel, he tells the story of Cupid and Psyche. Psyche was a merchant's daughter whose beauty aroused the jealousy of Venus; Venus ordered her son Cupid to make Psyche fall in love with a vile, deformed creature. But Cupid fell in love with her himself and every night would come to her. Eventually, however, Jupiter secured immortality for Psyche and so Cupid was united with her forever.

Keats had read the story in Apuleius and probably had seen reproductions of paintings of Cupid in the bedroom of Psyche. The subject was a very popular one with Renaissance and later artists. Keats' artist friends would have been familiar with it and might have drawn Keats' attention to reproductions.

What interested Keats particularly in the myth was the fact that Psyche, a mortal, achieved immortality through love. In *Endymion*, Keats has his hero achieve immortality through love; in *The Eve of St. Agnes*, Porphyro achieves a kind of immortality through love. Keats' ideal of perfect love was romantic love perpetuated. Psyche had achieved an immortality of erotic love. She had realized Keats' youthful dream of love. It was inevitable that he should have written his "Ode to Psyche."

Classical antiquity had not worshiped Psyche because it had no knowledge of her before Apuleius invented her. But in a poem, Keats could do on a small scale what classical antiquity had not done. He could build her a shrine in his imagination and, in it, he would leave one window open for Love to enter in just as Cupid, the god of Love in the story told by Apuleius, had entered Psyche's room every night and enjoyed the sweets of love with her.

The "Ode to Psyche" is an important poem among Keats' works because it embodies Keats' ideal of love, an ideal unattainable in this world but possibly attainable hereafter and certainly attainable in the imagination, which can build a shrine to Psyche with a window through which Keats may enter and enjoy a perfect union with the perfect woman. In the story of Psyche, Keats found an ideal vehicle for the expression of one of his profoundest yearnings. The "Ode to Psyche" is a poem about young, warm Keatsian love, much like that in *The Eve of St. Agnes*.

In addition to what the "Ode to Psyche" reveals to the reader about Keats, the poem contains an abundance of imagery felicitously phrased. Flowers are "cool-rooted." "Olympus' faded hierarchy" states succinctly the fate that has overtaken the religion of the Greeks and Romans. "Haunted forest boughs" expresses eloquently the classical practice of peopling nature with hosts of such lesser divinities as nymphs. Pines "murmur" in the wind. Fancy is a botanist-gardener who "breeding flowers, will never breed the same."

Psyche's wings in the ode ("thy lucent fans") are accounted for by the fact that, in Greek, *psyche* is the word for soul, and the soul was often represented as having the wings of a butterfly. Cupid also traditionally had wings.

Questions and Essay Topics

1. Read the story of Cupid and Psyche in Apuleius' *The Golden Ass*. Does Keats' ode owe much to Apuleius' account?

2. What does Keats say indirectly about the imagination in his "Ode to Psyche"?

3. How does the "Ode to Psyche" differ in stanza form and rhyme scheme from the odes that follow it?

4. Why does Keats use an outdoor setting for his "Ode to Psyche"?

5. Would it have served Keats' purpose to have told more about the story of Psyche and Cupid in his "Ode to Psyche"?

"Ode on a Grecian Urn"

Summary

Keats' imagined urn is addressed as if he were contemplating a real urn. It has survived intact from antiquity. It is a "sylvan historian" telling us a story, which the poet suggests by a series of questions. Who are these gods or men carved or painted on the urn? Who are these reluctant maidens? What is this mad pursuit? Why the struggle to escape? What is the explanation for the presence of musical instruments? Why this mad ecstasy?

Imagined melodies are lovelier than those heard by human ears. Therefore the poet urges the musician pictured on the urn to play on. His song can never end nor the trees ever shed their leaves. The lover on the urn can never win a kiss from his beloved, but his beloved can never lose her beauty. Happy are the trees on the urn, for they can never lose their leaves. Happy is the musician forever playing songs forever new. The lovers on the urn enjoy a love forever warm, forever panting, and forever young, far better than actual love, which eventually brings frustration and dissatisfaction.

Who are the people coming to perform a sacrifice? To what altar does the priest lead a garlanded heifer? What town do they come from? That town will forever remain silent and deserted.

Fair urn, Keats says, adorned with figures of men and maidens, trees and grass, you bring our speculations to a point at which thought leads nowhere, like meditation on eternity. After our generation is gone, you will still be here, a friend to man, telling him that beauty is truth and truth is beauty — that is all he knows on earth and all he needs to know.

Commentary

Keats has created a Greek urn in his mind and has decorated it with three scenes. The first is full of frenzied action and the actors are men, or gods, and maidens. Other figures, or possibly the male figures, are playing musical instruments. The maidens are probably the nymphs of classical mythology. The men or gods are smitten with love and are pursuing them. Keats, who loved classical mythology, had probably read stories of such love games. In Book II of his *Endymion,* he recounts Alpheus' pursuit of Arethusa, and in Book III he tells of Glaucus' pursuit of Scylla.

The second scene is developed in stanzas II and III. Under the trees a lover is serenading his beloved. In stanza I, Keats confined himself to suggesting a scene by questions. The second scene is not presented by means of questions but by means of description. We see a youth in a grove playing a musical instrument and hoping, it seems, for a kiss from his beloved. The scene elicits some thoughts on the function of art from Keats. Art gives a kind of permanence to reality. The youth, the maiden, and the musical instrument are, as it were, caught and held permanently by being pictured on the urn. And so Keats can take pleasure in the thought that the music will play on forever, and although the lover can never receive the desired kiss, the maiden can never grow older nor lose any of her beauty. The love that they enjoy is superior to human love which leaves behind "a heart high-sorrowful and cloy'd,/ A burning forehead, and a parching tongue." The aftermath of human love is satiety and dissatisfaction. In these two stanzas Keats imagines a state of perfect existence which is represented by the lovers pictured on the urn. Art arrests desirable experience at a point before it can become undesirable. This, Keats seems to be telling us, is one of the pleasurable contributions of art to man.

The third scene on Keats' urn is a group of people on their way to perform a sacrifice to some god. The sacrificial victim, a lowing heifer, is held by a priest. Instead of limiting himself to the sacrificial procession as another scene on his urn, Keats goes on to mention the town emptied of its inhabitants by the procession. The town is desolate and will forever be silent.

The final stanza contains the beauty-truth equation, the most controversial line in all the criticism of Keats' poetry. No critic's interpretation of the line satisfies any other critic, however, and no doubt they will continue to wrestle with the equation as long as the poem is read. In the stanza, Keats also makes two main comments on his urn. The urn teases him out of thought, as does eternity; that is, the problem of the effect of a work of art on time and life, or simply of what art does, is a perplexing one, as is the effort to grapple with the concept of eternity. Art's (imagined) arrest of time is a form of eternity and, probably, is what brought the word *eternity* into the poem.

The second thought is the truth-beauty equation. Through the poet's imagination, the urn has been able to preserve a temporary and happy condition in permanence, but it cannot do the same for Keats or his generation; old age will waste them and bring them woe. Yet the pictured urn can do something for them and for succeeding generations as long as it will last. It will bring them through its pictured beauty a vision of happiness (truth) of a kind available in eternity, in the hereafter, just as it has brought Keats a vision of happiness by means of sharing its existence empathically and bringing its scenes to emotional life through his imagination. All you know on earth and all you need to know in regard to beautiful works of art, whether urns or poems about urns, is that they give an inkling of the unchanging happiness to be realized in the hereafter. When Keats says "that is all ye know on earth," he is postulating an existence beyond earth.

Although Keats was not a particularly religious man, his meditation on the problem of happiness and its brief duration in the course of writing "Ode on a Grecian Urn" brought him a glimpse of heaven, a state of existence which his letters show he did think about. In his letter of November 22, 1817, to Benjamin Bailey, he mentioned "another favorite Speculation of mine, that we shall enjoy ourselves here after by having what we called happiness on Earth repeated in a finer tone and so repeated."

Questions and Essay Topics

1. Read some of the interpretations of the truth-beauty equation in Harvey T. Lyon's *Keats' Well-Read Urn*. Which one of them is the most persuasive?

2. Does the last stanza of the poem flow out of and summarize the preceding stanzas?

3. Why does Keats include the lines on the "deserted village" in the poem?

4. Are unheard melodies really sweeter than heard melodies? In what sense can Keats' assertion be true?

"Ode on Melancholy"

Summary

The reader is not to go to the underworld (Lethe), nor to drink wolf's-bane (a poison), nor to take nightshade (also a poison), nor to have anything to do with yew-berries, the beetle, the death-moth, and the owl (all symbolic of death). Death and all things associated with it numb the experience of anguish. When a melancholy mood comes to the individual, he should feed it by observing the beauty of roses, rainbows, and peonies. Or if the one he loves is angry, let him hold her hand and feed on the loveliness of her eyes. Melancholy dwells with beauty, "beauty that must die," joy, and pleasure. It is to be found at the very heart of delight, but only the strongly sensuous man perceives it there. He is the one who can have the deepest experience of melancholy.

Commentary

The "Ode to Melancholy" belongs to a class of eighteenth-century poems that have some form of melancholy as their theme. Such poetry came to be called the "Graveyard School of Poetry" and the best-known example of it is Thomas Gray's "Elegy in a Country Churchyard." The romantic poets inherited this tradition. One of the effects of this somber poetry about death, graveyards, the brevity of pleasure and of life was a pleasing feeling of melancholy.

Keats' special variation on the theme was to make the claim that the keenest experience of melancholy was to be obtained not from death but from the contemplation of beautiful objects because they were fated to die. Therefore the most sensuous man, the man who can "burst Joy's grape against his palate fine," as Keats put it in a striking image, is capable of the liveliest response to melancholy. Keats' own experience of life and his individual temperament made him acutely aware of the close relationship between joy and sorrow. His happiness was constantly being chipped away by frustration. He was himself a very sensuous individual. In the "Ode to Melancholy," Keats, instead of rejecting melancholy, shows a healthy attraction toward it, for unless one keenly experiences it, he cannot appreciate joy.

The abruptness with which "Ode to Melancholy" begins is accounted for by the fact that the stanza with which the poem begins was originally the second stanza. The original first stanza was

> Though you should build a bark of dead men's bones,
>   And rear a phantom gibbet for a mast,
> Stitch creeds together for a sail, with groans
>   To fill it out, blood-stained and aghast;
> Although your rudder be a dragon's tail
>   Long sever'd, yet still hard with agony,
>   Your cordage large uprootings from the skull
> Of bald Medusa, certes you would fail
>   To find the Melancholy — whether she
>   Dreameth in any isle of Lethe dull.

We don't know why Keats rejected this original beginning stanza, but we can guess. He was straining to create images of death that would convey something of the repulsiveness of death — to give the reader a romantic shudder of the Gothic kind — and what he succeeded in doing was repulsive instead of delicately suggestive and was out of keeping with what he achieved in the rest of the poem. Moreover, he may have felt that two stanzas on death were more than enough. The stanza is crude and Keats realized it.

The stanza with which Keats decided to begin the poem is startling, but not crude. Keats brought together a remarkable collection of objects in the stanza. Lethe is a river in the classical underworld. Wolfsbane and nightshade are poisonous plants. The yew-berry is the seed (also poisonous) of the yewtree, which, because it is hardy and an evergreen, is traditionally planted in English graveyards. Replicas of a black beetle were frequently placed in tombs by Egyptians; to the Egyptians, the scarab or black beetle was a symbol of resurrection, but to Keats they were a symbol of death because of their association with tombs. The death-moth or butterfly represented the soul leaving the body at death. The owl was often associated with otherworldly symbols because of its nocturnal habits and its ominous hooting. Death is the common denominator of the displays in Keats' museum of natural history. The language of the stanza is vastly superior to that of the discarded stanza. Nothing in it can compare with calling nightshade the "ruby grape of Proserpine," the queen of the underworld, nor with making a rosary of yew-berries and thereby automatically suggesting prayers for the dying or the dead. The stanza is one of the richest and strangest in Keats' poetry.

Questions and Essay Topics

1. Look up other poems on melancholy in eighteenth-century poetry and compare them with the "Ode on Melancholy."

2. Is the "Ode on Melancholy" as philosophical a poem as the other odes?

3. Examine the ritual element in the last stanza of the poem. Is it in keeping with the rest of the poem?

4. Do Keats' other poems reveal a tendency toward melancholy in him?

"Ode to a Nightingale"

Summary

Keats is in a state of uncomfortable drowsiness. Envy of the imagined happiness of the nightingale is not responsible for his condition; rather, it is a reaction to the happiness he has experienced through sharing in the happiness of the nightingale. The bird's happiness is conveyed in its singing.

Keats longs for a draught of wine which would take him out of himself and allow him to join his existence with that of the bird. The wine would put him in a state in which he would no longer be himself, aware that life is full of pain, that the young die, the old suffer, and that just to think about life brings sorrow and despair. But wine is not needed to enable him to escape. His imagination will serve just as well. As soon as he realizes this, he is, in spirit, lifted up above the trees and can see the moon and the stars even though where he is physically there is only a glimmering of light. He cannot see what flowers are growing around him, but from their odor and from his knowledge of what flowers should be in bloom at the time he can guess.

In the darkness he listens to the nightingale. Now, he feels, it would be a rich experience to die, "to cease upon the midnight with no pain" while the bird would continue to sing ecstatically. Many a time, he confesses, he has been "half in love with easeful Death." The nightingale is free from the human fate of having to die. The song of the nightingale that he is listening to was heard in ancient times by emperor and peasant. Perhaps even Ruth (whose story is told in the Old Testament) heard it.

"Forlorn," the last word of the preceding stanza, brings Keats in the concluding stanza back to consciousness of what he is and where he is. He cannot escape even with the help of the imagination. The singing of the bird grows fainter and dies away. The experience he has had seems so strange and confusing that he is not sure whether it was a vision or a daydream. He is even uncertain whether he is asleep or awake.

Commentary

The "Ode to a Nightingale" is a regular ode. All eight stanzas have ten pentameter lines and a uniform rhyme scheme. Although the poem is regular in form, it leaves the impression of being a kind of rhapsody; Keats is allowing his thoughts and emotions free expression. One thought suggests another and, in this way, the poem proceeds to a somewhat arbitrary conclusion. The poem impresses the reader as being the result of free inspiration uncontrolled by a preconceived plan. The poem is Keats in the act of sharing with the reader an experience he is having rather than recalling an experience. The experience is not entirely coherent. It is what happens in his mind while he is listening to the song of a nightingale.

Three main thoughts stand out in the ode. One is Keats' evaluation of life; life is a vale of tears and frustration. The happiness which Keats hears in the song of the nightingale has made him happy momentarily but has been succeeded by a feeling of torpor which in turn is succeeded by the conviction that life is not only painful but also intolerable. His taste of happiness in hearing the nightingale has made him all the more aware of the unhappiness of life. Keats wants to escape from life, not by means of wine, but by a much more powerful agent, the imagination.

The second main thought and the main theme of the poem is Keats' wish that he might die and be rid of life altogether, providing he could die as easily and painlessly as he could fall asleep. The preoccupation with death does not seem to have been caused by any turn for the worse in Keats' fortunes at the time he wrote the ode (May, 1819). In many respects Keats' life had been unsatisfactory for some time before he wrote the poem. His family life was shattered by the departure of one brother to America and the death from tuberculosis of the other. His second volume of poetry had been harshly reviewed. He had no gainful occupation and no prospects, since he had abandoned his medical studies. His financial condition was insecure. He had not been well in the fall and winter of 1818-19 and possibly he was already suffering from tuberculosis. He could not marry

Fanny Brawne because he was not in a position to support her. Thus the death-wish in the ode may be a reaction to a multitude of troubles and frustrations, all of which were still with him. The heavy weight of life pressing down on him forced "Ode to a Nightingale" out of him. Keats more than once expressed a desire for "easeful Death," yet when he was in the final stages of tuberculosis he fought against death by going to Italy where he hoped the climate would cure him. The death-wish in the ode is a passing but recurrent attitude toward a life that was unsatisfactory in so many ways.

The third main thought in the ode is the power of imagination or fancy. (Keats does not make any clear-cut distinction between the two.) In the ode Keats rejects wine for poetry, the product of imagination, as a means of identifying his existence with that of the happy nightingale. But poetry does not work the way it is supposed to. He soon finds himself back with his everyday, trouble-filled self. That "fancy cannot cheat so well/ As she is fam'd to do," he admits in the concluding stanza. The imagination is not the all-powerful function Keats, at times, thought it was. It cannot give more than a temporary escape from the cares of life.

Keats' assignment of immortality to the nightingale in stanza VII has caused readers much trouble. Keats perhaps was thinking of a literal nightingale; more likely, however, he was thinking of the nightingale as a symbol of poetry, which has a permanence.

Keats' evocative power is shown especially in stanza II where he associates a beaker of wine "with beaded bubbles winking at the brim," with sunny France and the "sunburnt mirth" of the harvesters, and in his picture in stanza VII of Ruth suffering from homesickness "amid the alien corn." The whole ode is a triumph of tonal richness of that adagio verbal music that is Keats' special contribution to the many voices of poetry.

Questions and Essay Topics

1. Look up *nightingale* in a handbook of ornithology and in a handbook of mythology. Why do poets sometimes describe the nightingale's song as sad or "plaintive"?

2. What does Keats mean by "charm'd magic casements . . . in faery lands forlorn"?

3. Read the story of Ruth in the Old Testament. What does Keats' allusion add to the meaning of the poem?

4. Do you think the concluding stanza of the poem is on the same level of excellence as the other stanzas? Is it a good ending for the poem?

5. The form of Keats' odes is said to have resulted from his study of the sonnet. In what way are they indebted to the sonnet?

Lamia

Summary

Part I

The god Hermes (Mercury), having fallen deeply in love with a nymph who has hidden herself from him, hears a voice complaining of being imprisoned in a snake's body. The speaker is a beautiful serpent. She tells Hermes that she knows he seeks a nymph and offers to make the nymph, to whom she has given the power of invisibility, visible to him providing he will restore to her her woman's body. Hermes gladly agrees. The nymph becomes visible to Hermes; the serpent turns into a beautiful woman and disappears.

Lamia, the serpent-turned-woman, while in her serpent state, had the power to send her spirit wherever she wished. On one of her spirit journeys she had seen a Corinthian youth, Lycius. Now, as woman, she reappears and stands at the side of a road along which she knows Lycius will come on his way to

Corinth. When he arrives, she addresses him, asking him if he will leave her all alone where she is. Lycius looks at her and at once falls violently in love with her. Together they walk to Corinth and make their abode in a mansion which she leads him to. There they live together as man and wife, avoiding the company of others.

Part II

Lycius and Lamia live happily in the blisses of love until Lycius decides they ought to marry and invite all their friends to the marriage festival. Lamia is strongly opposed to this plan, but the persistence of Lycius at last wins her reluctant consent. She agrees on the condition that Lycius will not invite the philosopher Apollonius to the marriage feast.

While Lycius is absent inviting all his kinsfolk to the wedding, Lamia, with her magic powers, summons invisible servants who decorate the banquet room and furnish it with rich foods of every kind. When Lycius' guests arrive — Lamia has no friends or relatives in Corinth, she tells Lycius — they marvel at the splendor of the mansion. None of them had known that there was such a magnificent palace in Corinth. Among the guests is Apollonius, who has come uninvited.

At the height of the wedding feast, Apollonius begins to stare fixedly at Lamia. Lamia grows pale and exhibits extreme discomfort. She makes no answer to Lycius' agonized questions as to what ails her. The feasting and the music come to a stop. Turning to Apollonius, Lycius commands him to cease staring at Lamia. "Fool," answers the philosopher contemptuously, "from every ill/ Of life have I preserv'd thee to this day,/ And shall I see thee made a serpent's prey?" Looking at Lamia again, he utters two words: "A serpent!" At the words, Lamia vanishes. At the moment of her disappearance, Lycius dies.

Commentary

Lamia is the last of the four metrical romances written by Keats. Its source is a short anecdote in Robert Burton's *Anatomy of Melancholy* that Keats appended at the end of the poem. As Keats was intending to write a poem that would have popular appeal in *Lamia*, it is possible that his intention was merely to expand the anecdote into a lengthy tale by means of the rich sensuous detail which is the special hallmark of *The Eve of St. Agnes*. *Lamia* has puzzled critics because of the elusiveness of its theme. *Lamia* seems to say that passionate love is an illusion and an enchantment, ultimately destructive. On the other hand, Keats' attitude toward his characters is somewhat ambiguous. Lamia is not entitled to human love because she is not human; she is a serpent. She has deceived Lycius. She must be kept a secret. She has no family, no parents. She does not want Apollonius invited to the marriage because she fears he will expose her. Nevertheless, Keats presents her sympathetically; she is not an evil creature.

Lycius too is presented sympathetically but in living with Lamia he is indulging in "sweet sin." Since he is a high-minded Platonist when first introduced into the story, his love for Lamia is indulging a weakness. When Lycius and Lamia meet Apollonius, Lycius' mentor, while walking through Corinth, Lycius is at pains to avoid being recognized by him.

In lines 375-76, Part I, Lycius calls Apollonius "my trusty guide/ And good instructor" and in lines 296-97, Part II, Apollonius makes the claim that "from every ill/ Of life have I preserv'd thee to this day." Yet Apollonius in the story seems malignant and scornful of Lycius, whose death he is indirectly responsible for.

Keats may be presenting a situation dramatically in *Lamia*, showing the good and the bad, and not coming to any final judgment. But he seems to be doing more than that. The subject of *Lamia* is consuming love such as Keats himself was experiencing when he wrote the poem. His letters to Fanny Brawne indicate that he was obsessed by her beauty—and, at the same time, fearful for his freedom. He realized, however, that desire must be curbed by restraint, that love must harmonize with, and be a part of life, rather than dominate and control it. *Lamia*, therefore, can be regarded as a warning against the all-absorbing nature of illusory, passionate love and a recognition of the claims of reason.

The reason why *Lamia* is usually not included in the first rank among Keats' poems may be that the story it tells is not of absorbing interest. It lacks suspense, but in this respect it is not inferior to *The Eve of St. Agnes,* which also has relatively little suspense. Neither poem has much in the way of crisis and climax. Keats makes more use of dialogue in *Lamia* than in *The Eve of St. Agnes,* and in this area his narrative technique is superior, but this is to be expected since *Lamia* has more characters than *The Eve of St. Agnes.* The great advantage that *The Eve of St. Agnes* has over *Lamia* is that it is about human lovers. A tale about the love between a supernatural creature like Lamia and a human being may have romantic strangeness but it does not have much human interest. In richness of description, however, *Lamia* is probably as good as anything Keats wrote. Lamia-as-snake is as beautiful as Lamia-as-woman:

> She was a gordian shape of dazzling hue,
> Vermilion-spotted, golden, green, and blue;
> Striped like a zebra, freckled like a pard,
> Eyed like a peacock, and all crimson barr'd;
> And full of silver moons, that, as she breathed,
> Dissolv'd or brighter shone, or interwreathed
> Their lustres with the gloomier tapestries — I, 47-53

Just as in *The Eve of St. Agnes* Keats concentrated on the stained glass window in order to emphasize the loveliness of Madeline, so in *Lamia* Keats devotes many lines of description to the banquet hall in the palace of Lamia and Lycius in order to emphasize their tragedy, for it was there that Lamia vanished and Lycius perished. The banquet hall is the setting of the climax of the story.

For his last narrative poem, Keats used the iambic pentameter couplets of *Endymion,* but he shows a much greater mastery of his couplets in *Lamia* than in *Endymion.* He does not let the rhymes control the sense, and the lines flow on so smoothly that the reader is almost unaware of the rhymes. To vary his couplets, he uses triplets and iambic hexameter lines.

Questions and Essay Topics

1. Find out all you can about the lamia. Are lamias always evil creatures in folklore?

2. Read Keats' source in Robert Burton's *Anatomy of Melancholy*. Does Keats follow his source closely?

3. Is the tragic ending of *Lamia* inevitable?

4. Is Lamia a "fatal woman" like "la belle dame sans merci"?

5. Should Keats have had Lycius die in *Lamia*?

"To Autumn"

Summary

Autumn joins with the maturing sun to load the vines with grapes, to ripen apples and other fruit, "swell the gourd," fill up the hazel shells, and set budding more and more flowers. Autumn may be seen sitting on a threshing floor, sound asleep in a grain field filled with poppies, carrying a load of grain across a brook, or watching the juice oozing from a cider press. The sounds of autumn are the wailing of gnats, the bleating of lambs, the singing of hedge crickets, the whistling of robins, and the twittering of swallows.

Commentary

"To Autumn" is one of the last poems written by Keats. His method of developing the poem is to heap up imagery typical of autumn. His autumn is early autumn, when all the products of nature have reached a state of perfect maturity. Autumn is personified and is perceived in a state of activity. In the first stanza, autumn is a friendly conspirator working with the sun to bring fruits to a state of perfect fullness and ripeness. In the second stanza, autumn is a thresher sitting on a granary floor, a reaper asleep in a grain field, a gleaner crossing a brook, and, lastly, a cider maker. In the final stanza, autumn is seen as a musician, and the music which autumn produces is as pleasant as the music of spring—the sounds of gnats, lambs, crickets, robins and swallows.

In the first stanza, Keats concentrates on the sights of autumn, ripening grapes and apples, swelling gourds and hazel nuts, and blooming flowers. In the second stanza, the emphasis is on the characteristic activities of autumn, threshing, reaping, gleaning, and cider making. In the concluding stanza, the poet puts the emphasis on the sounds of autumn, produced by insects, animals, and birds. To his ears, this music is just as sweet as the music of spring.

The ending of the poem is artistically made to correspond with the ending of a day: "And gathering swallows twitter in the skies." In the evening, swallows gather in flocks preparatory to returning to their nests for the night.

"To Autumn" is sometimes called an ode, but Keats does not call it one. However, its structure and rhyme scheme are similar to those of his odes of the spring of 1819, and, like those odes, it is remarkable for its richness of imagery. It is a feast of sights and sounds.

Questions and Essay Topics

1. Is "To Autumn" a purely descriptive poem?

2. Is "clammy" a suitable word for describing cells filled with honey?

3. Compare Keats' "To Autumn" with the autumn section of *The Seasons*, a popular poem by the eighteenth-century poet James Thomson. Do you think Thomson could have influenced Keats in "To Autumn"?

SELECTED BIBLIOGRAPHY

Biography

BATE, W. J. *John Keats.* Cambridge: Harvard University Press, 1963. Best biography. Comments on many poems.

WARD, AILEEN. *John Keats: The Making of a Poet.* New York: Viking Press, 1963. Excellent biography.

Editions

DE SELINCOURT, E., ed. *The Poems of John Keats,* 7th ed. London: Methuen, 1951. Best one-volume edition of Keats' poetry.

FORMAN, H. B., ed., revisions by M. B. FORMAN. *The Poetical Works and Other Writings of John Keats,* 7 vols. New York: Scribner's, 1938-39.

GARROD, H. W., ed. *Poetical Works.* London, New York: Oxford University Press, 1958. Variorum edition of Keats' poems.

Reference and Criticism

FINNEY, C. L. *The Evolution of Keats' Poetry,* 2 vols. New York: Russell & Russell, 1963. Contains much information of every kind about Keats' poems.

MUIR, KENNETH, ed. *John Keats: A Reassessment.* Liverpool: Liverpool University Press, 1958.

MURRY, J. M. *Keats,* 4th ed. New York: Noonday Press, 1955.

PETTET, E. C. *On the Poetry of Keats.* Cambridge: Cambridge University Press, 1957. Best book on Keats' poetry.

SLOTE, BERNICE. *Keats and the Dramatic Principle.* Lincoln: University of Nebraska Press, 1958.

THORPE, C. D. *The Mind of John Keats.* New York: Russell & Russell, 1964.

WASSERMAN, E. R. *The Finer Tone: Keats' Major Poems.* Baltimore: Johns Hopkins University Press, 1953.

Shelley Notes

LIFE OF SHELLEY

Percy Bysshe Shelley was born at Field Place, Sussex, in 1792, the son of a well-to-do landowner. At the age of ten, he was sent to Syon House Academy near London. There he was bullied and often lonely, but there too he acquired an interest in science, especially astronomy and chemistry, and became an avid reader of juvenile thrillers filled with horrors of various kinds. Shelley reacted to the bullying he was subjected to with violent anger and a determination to devote himself to opposing every form of tyranny.

In 1804, Shelley entered Eton College, where he encountered more of the same bullying he had been subjected to at Syon House. His outbursts of rage and his inability to fight encouraged the other boys to provoke him. He became known as "Mad Shelley" because of his rather unconventional behavior. However, he made a number of friends at Eton and embarked on his literary career. His "Gothic" horror novel, *Zastrozzi*, was published in 1810. In the same year, with his sister, he co-authored a volume of poems, most of them in the Gothic tradition, entitled *Original Poetry by Victor* [Shelley] *and Cazire* [Elizabeth Shelley]. It was also in 1810 that Shelley began his short career at Oxford University. And, in addition, he published a second Gothic novel of terror, *St. Irvyne*, most of which he had written at Eton. A short volume of poems, *Posthumous Fragments of Margaret Nicholson,* purporting to be edited by a John Fitz-Victor, was also published by Shelley in 1810. A third publication, a pamphlet entitled *The Necessity of Atheism,* brought Shelley's university career to an abrupt end. On March 25, 1811, he was summoned to appear before the master of University College and, when he refused to admit or deny his authorship of the pamphlet, he was immediately expelled.

Shortly after his expulsion, he eloped to Scotland with Harriet Westbrook, a schoolgirl companion of his sister, Hellen. Shelley's marriage further alienated him from his father, whose pride had been deeply hurt by Shelley's expulsion from Oxford. Shelley and his young wife drifted from one locality to another, living precariously on whatever money they could borrow. Eventually Shelley's father settled an allowance on him. During this period Shelley continued to read incessantly. His reading helped to confirm him in the radical political and social opinions he had acquired.

In February, 1812, Shelley and Harriet were in Ireland distributing Shelley's pamphlet, *Address to the Irish People*. In this publication, Shelley urged virtue on the Irish, who were living in misery because of the English Parliament. The remedy for their wrongs, he told the Irish people, was to be found in the practice of sobriety, moderation, and wisdom. As soon as virtue prevailed, government must succumb because government's only excuse for existing was the absence of virtue.

Toward the middle of 1813, Shelley's first poem of any merit, *Queen Mab*, made its appearance. *Queen Mab* incorporated many of Shelley's radical ideas. To Shelley, Christianity was the worst of tyrannies. God was an evil creature of the human mind. Priests, kings, and commerce were sources of evil. Marriage was a form of tyranny. The eating of meat was a cause of human vices.

A major turning point in Shelley's life occurred in July, 1814, when he eloped to the continent with Mary Godwin, the daughter of the radical philosopher William Godwin, author of *Political Justice*. Shelley, who did not believe in marriage, had convinced himself that his wife Harriet, now the mother of two children, no longer supplied him with the complete sympathy he craved and that Mary did. It is characteristic of Shelley's sometimes blind idealism that he invited Harriet to live with Mary and himself; she refused, however, but Shelley could never understand her unwillingness to do so. The months that followed were difficult ones for Shelley. The elopement had cost him the loss of old friends, including Mary's father, and he was in constant financial difficulties. He even went so far as to ask Harriet for money to avoid being arrested for debt.

The difficulties of Shelley's life in 1814 and 1815 interfered with the writing of poetry. Not until February, 1816, did he publish a poem that was on a par with *Queen Mab*. In that month appeared a volume in which "Alastor" was the major poem. The theme of "Alastor" is that concentration on high ideals has the effect of making the world seem dark and ugly. The volume, however, received little critical notice, and even that was unfriendly.

In May, 1816, Shelley and Mary, who had been living in England, left for the Continent. The death of Shelley's wealthy grandfather made Shelley financially independent on an income of £1000 a year, the chief drain on which was the endless necessity of helping Mary's father out of his recurrent financial difficulties. In Switzerland, Shelley met Byron, who had left England only ten days before Shelley. The two developed a warm friendship which lasted until Shelley's death. The months that they spent together in Switzerland were among the happiest in Shelley's life. They found each other's company very stimulating. It was at this time that Byron wrote the third, and best, canto of *Childe Harold's Pilgrimage* and Mary wrote her famous *Frankenstein*. This almost idyllic period in Shelley's life came to an end when Shelley had to return to England to take care of money matters in late August, 1816. Two calamities befell him shortly after his return to England: the suicide of Fanny Imlay, Mary's half sister and a member of the Godwin household, and, shortly after, the suicide of his wife Harriet. Shelley tried to gain custody of his two children but was denied it by a decision of the Lord Chancellor. On December 29, 1816, he legalized his association with Mary by marrying her.

Shelley's longest poem, *The Revolt of Islam*, in part a heavily symbolic account of a bloodless revolution, and in part a restatement of the radical social views of *Queen Mab*, was the work of more than half of 1817. It is not only Shelley's longest poem, but it is also one of his least readable poems, partly because of its symbolism and partly because of its structural weakness. Besides writing *The Revolt of Islam* in 1817, Shelley also wrote "Rosalind and Helen," the story of two pairs of lovers, one pair of which appears to be Shelley and Mary, whose love without marriage is justified.

In 1818, Shelley left England for Italy, never to return. During that summer, he occupied himself in reading and translating Plato's *Symposium*. Following a journey to Venice, where Shelley visited Byron, the Shelleys suffered a severe loss in the death of their little daughter, Clara. The death of Clara caused a strain to develop between Shelley and his wife, Mary, who felt that the journey to Venice, which was made on the insistence of Shelley, was responsible for the death of their daughter. Shelley's "Julian and Maddalo," written in the fall of 1818, reflects this tension.

After spending the winter of 1818-19 in Naples, the Shelleys moved on to Rome, where they remained from March to June, 1819. The year 1819 proved to be Shelley's *annus mirabilis*. He completed *Prometheus Unbound*, the embodiment of his dream of a brave new world; he composed his play, *The Cenci*, a study in human wickedness which is probably the best play written by a romantic poet; and he began a political pamphlet entitled *A Philosophical View of Reform*, in which he made some practical suggestions for political reforms in England; in addition, he wrote a number of short poems on the political situation in England, which he was convinced bordered on revolution. In these poems, as well as in *Prometheus* and *The Cenci*, oppression is exposed and attacked. 1819 was also a sad year for the Shelleys; their only surviving child, William, died in Rome early in June.

In June, 1819, the Shelleys left Rome for Leghorn, where they remained until October. In October, they moved to Florence so that Mary, who was pregnant, could be near a doctor she had confidence in. Mary's last child, Percy Florence, the only one who lived to maturity, was born on November 2. Late in January, 1820, the Shelleys were again on the move. This time their destination was Pisa. The Shelleys lived either in or near Pisa until Shelley's death in 1822.

The Cenci was Shelley's last long poem. The poetry that he wrote in Pisa was either short pieces or poems of a few hundred lines. As was his custom, he read continually, partly to keep his mind stimulated and partly because he was a reader by nature. His reading, however, does not seem to have been undertaken as a preparation for writing such a great poem as Milton's *Paradise Lost*. Outstanding among his Pisan poems are "Epipsychidion," a work in which he extols the charms of Emilia Viviani, the young daughter of the governor of Pisa, and *Adonais*, an elegy in which he laments the death of John Keats and, at the same time, attacks the critics who had heaped opprobrium on himself and had, Shelley thought, been the cause of the death of Keats. A good deal of the poetry of his last years is marked by melancholy. Both Shelley and his wife were subject to periodic attacks of depression. The melancholy in Shelley's last poems is probably due to a feeling that a rift had developed between himself and his wife and also to the conviction that his attempt to improve the world through poetry had not succeeded to any noticeable degree. The critics remained hostile.

In spite of Shelley's growing disenchantment with the world, he experienced some of the deepest happiness of his life during his last months. Ironically, this happiness was associated with the boat in which he met his death. At the end of April, 1822, the Shelleys and their friends the Williamses rented a house in San Terenzo, a village on the Gulf of Spezia, not far from Pisa. To San Terenzo they brought a boat, the *Don Juan*, built for them in Genoa according to Edward Williams' specifications. Shelley and Williams found the boat completely satisfactory and a constant source of delight. On the eighth of July, as the *Don Juan* was carrying the two friends from Leghorn to San Terenzo, a heavy squall suddenly came up and the *Don Juan* disappeared from sight. Several days later, the bodies of Shelley and Williams were washed up on the shores of the Bay of Lerici. The body of Shelley was cremated and the ashes buried in the Protestant Cemetery in Rome, not far from the grave of Keats.

SUMMARIES AND COMMENTARIES

"Hymn to Intellectual Beauty"

Summary

The shadow of a strange power floats unseen throughout the world, entering into man, coming and going mysteriously. Shelley asks this shadow, which he calls a "Spirit of Beauty," where it has gone and why it disappears and leaves us desolate. Then he acknowledges that it is vain to ask this question; one might as well ask why rainbows disappear or why man can both love and hate, despair and hope. No voice from another world has ever answered these questions. The "names of Demon, Ghost, and Heaven" are the record of men's vain attempts to get answers to such questions. Only the light of the Spirit of Beauty gives grace and truth to the restless dream which life is. If the Spirit of Beauty remained constantly with man, man would be immortal and omnipotent. It nourishes human thought. The poet beseeches this spirit not to depart from the world. Without it, death would be an experience to be feared.

When Shelley was a boy, he sought spiritual reality in ghosts and the dead. In his search, the shadow of the Spirit of Beauty suddenly fell on him and filled him with elation. He vowed that he would dedicate himself to this Spirit and he has kept his vow. He is convinced that it will free the world from the state of slavery in which it is. He prays that this power will bring calm to his life, for he worships it. It has taught him to fear himself and love all mankind.

Commentary

The "Hymn to Intellectual Beauty" was conceived and written during a boating excursion with Byron on Lake Geneva, Switzerland, in June, 1816. The beauty of the lake and of the Swiss Alps is responsible for Shelley's elevating what he calls "Intellectual Beauty" to the ruling priniciple of the universe.

Alpine scenery was new to Shelley and unutterably beautiful. He was profoundly moved by it, and the poem, he wrote to Leigh Hunt, was "composed under the influence of feelings which agitated me even to tears." Thanks to the Alps, Shelley, who had given up Christianity, had at last found a deity which he could wholeheartedly adore. The worship of beauty is Shelley's new religion, and it is significant that he calls his poem a hymn, a term used almost exclusively for religious verse. Later, in August, 1817, Shelley read Plato's *Symposium* and his faith in beauty was no doubt strengthened by Plato's discussion of abstract beauty in that work and in the *Phaedrus*, which Shelley read in August, 1818. It was daily intercourse with stunning beauty, not Plato, however, that brought Shelley to his new faith. Joseph Barrell, in his *Shelley and the Thought of His Time: A Study in the History of Ideas*, makes it abundantly clear that the "Hymn" is not Platonic.

The central thought of "Hymn to Intellectual Beauty" is that there is a spiritual power that stands apart from both the physical world and the heart of man. This power is unknown to man and invisible, but its shadow visits "this various world with as inconstant wing/ As summer winds that creep from flower to flower" and it visits also "with inconstant glance/ Each human heart and countenance." When it passes away it leaves "our state,/ This dim vast vale of tears, vacant and desolate." Shelley does not profess to know why Intellectual Beauty, which he calls "unknown and awful," is an inconstant visitor, but he is convinced that if it kept "with [its] glorious train firm state" within man's heart, man would be "immortal and omnipotent." But since the Spirit of Beauty visits the world and man's heart with such irregularity, Shelley pleads with his deity rather than praises it. It remains remote and inaccessible. In the concluding stanza Shelley is a suppliant praying that the power of the Spirit of Beauty will continue to supply its calm "to one who worships thee,/ And every form containing thee."

In Stanza V, Shelley confesses that as a boy, while he was searching for spiritual reality (chiefly by reading Gothic romances, it would appear), the shadow of Intellectual Beauty suddenly fell on him. He shrieked and clasped his hands in ecstasy. As a consequence of this experience, he tells us in Stanza VI, he vowed that he would dedicate his "powers/ To thee and thine," and he has kept his vow. The experience also left him with the hope that the Spirit of Beauty would free "this world from its dark slavery." In this stanza, Shelley seems to combine two of the major interests of his life, love of beauty and love of freedom.

In regard to the "Intellectual Beauty" of the title, Barrell remarks that it implies an approach by means of the mental faculties but that Shelley probably meant to convey the idea that his concept of beauty was abstract rather than concrete. His approach is romantic and emotional. Shelley, however, seems to think of his Spirit of Beauty as personal, like the God of Christianity. He addresses it, pleads with it, worships it, but he may be using only the rhetorical device of personification.

The "Hymn to Intellectual Beauty" is more remarkable for what it tells us about Shelley than it is as a work of art. By his very nature, Shelley was an idealist and no form of materialism could appeal to him more than temporarily.

Questions and Essay Topics

1. Compare Shelley's concept of deity in the "Hymn" to his concept of deity in *Adonais*.

2. Consult Shelley's biography for an account of his early reading.

3. Trace Shelley's spiritual development.

4. Why does Shelley call beauty "intellectual"? Can it be experienced only through the mind?

5. In what way is Shelley's "Hymn" related to his social and political ideals?

6. Is Shelley's Intellectual Beauty abstract or concrete?

"Ozymandias"

Summary

A traveller tells the poet that two huge stone legs stand in the desert. Near them on the sand lies a damaged stone head. The face is distinguished by a frown and a sneer which the sculptor carved on the features. On the pedestal are inscribed the words "My name is Ozymandias, king of kings:/ Look on my works, ye Mighty, and despair!" Around the huge fragments stretches the empty desert.

Commentary

Shelley's irregular sonnet on the fragments of a huge statue of an Egyptian pharaoh begins with a statement that arouses the interest of the reader at once:

> I met a traveller from an antique land
> Who said: Two vast and trunkless legs of stone
> Stand in the desert.

The mention of a traveller is a promise of a story. The story is a characteristically Shelleyan one about tyranny and how time makes a mockery of the boastfulness of even the most powerful kings. The story is over and Shelley's point is made before the reader realizes that he has been subjected to a moral lesson.

The fine beginning is followed by a condensed and vigorous account of what the traveller saw in addition to the two huge legs standing in the desert: a shattered visage, a pedestal, and on it a boastful inscription. Nothing more except the empty desert. Shelley puts the words of the inscription in effectively ironic contrast with the surroundings. The rulers of the world, "ye Mighty," are told by Ozymandias, "king of kings," to look upon his works and despair of emulating them. Now one looks and sees nothing whatsoever. Instead of the architectural marvels promised by the inscription, "the lone and level sands stretch far away." Just as the sculptor mocked Ozymandias by putting on the face of the colossal monument a "frown/ And wrinkled lip, and sneer of cold command," so time has also mocked him by reducing his vain boast to nothingness. The works that were to be the despair of other pharaohs have completely disappeared. Even the gigantic statue of himself that he had commissioned has been reduced to two legs, a shattered face, and a pedestal.

"Ozymandias" was written by Shelley in competition with his friend Horace Smith. The superiority of Shelley's choice of details and of the vigor of his diction are splendidly illustrated by a comparison with the octave of his friend's sonnet:

> In Egypt's sandy silence, all alone
> Stands a gigantic leg, which far off throws
> The only shadow that the desert knows.
> "I am Great Ozymandias," saith the stone,
> "The king of kings; this mighty city shows
> The wonders of my hand." The city's gone!
> Nought but the leg remaining to disclose
> The site of that forgotten Babylon.

Both poets remove the city of Thebes, the site of the statue, from their poems for artistic purposes.

Ozymandias was the name by which Rameses II, a pharaoh famous for the number of architectural structures he caused to be erected, was known to the Greeks. Shelley had read of the statue in Diodorus Siculus, a Roman writer, who had described it as intact. He had obviously read about it in some other source also since he knew that the statue was no longer intact. The problem of Shelley's sources is discussed in an interesting, illustrated article by Johnstone Parr, "Shelley's 'Ozymandias,'" *Keats-Shelley Journal,* Vol. VI (1957).

Questions and Essay Topics

1. Look up a brief account of Rameses II (Ozymandias).

2. What point in regard to tyranny is Shelley making in the sonnet?

3. Why is "Ozymandias" said to be an irregular sonnet?

"Stanzas Written in Dejection, near Naples"

Summary

The day is warm, the sky is clear, the waves sparkle. Blue islands and snow-topped mountains look purple in the midday light. Buds are ready to blossom. The sounds of the winds, the birds, the waves, and of Naples itself blend in pleasant harmony. Shelley sees the seaweed on the ocean bottom and watches the waves dissolve into light as they strike the shore. He sits alone on the sand, observing the sparkling ocean and listening to the sound of the waves. How pleasant all this would be if there were someone with whom he could share the emotion he feels.

Unfortunately, Shelley lacks hope, health, peace, calmness, contentment, fame, power, love, and leisure. He sees others who enjoy all these and find life a pleasure. It is otherwise with him. He would like to lie down like a tired child and "weep away the life of care" which he has endured and must continue to endure. Death would steal upon him quietly, turning his warm cheeks cold while the waves continued their monotonous rhythm as conciousness grew fainter. Some might mourn his death just as he will regret the departure of this beautiful day to which his melancholy is in contrast. He is not popular, but nevertheless they might mourn his death while disapproving of his life. The end of this day will not bring mixed feelings to him, however. Since it has been enjoyed, it will live on in his memory.

Commentary

Shelley's state of dejection in "Stanzas" is artistically placed in a sharply contrasting setting that effectively emphasizes the dejection. Shelley implies that no matter how much harmony there may exist between nature and man, man must be in a condition to be able to find pleasure in that harmony. Shelley was far from being in such a condition. Newman Ivey White, the author of the definitive life of Shelley, writes that Shelley was so depressed while in Naples that it is said that he tried to commit suicide *(Shelley,* Vol. II, p. 78).

Shelley was in Naples from November 29, 1818, to February 28, 1819. Naples in winter offers a pleasantly warm climate. Naples is at its best, so far as weather is concerned, and Shelley and his wife, Mary, should have been happy there. However, Shelley was in poor health and the delightful winter climate of Naples did not help him. The major cause of his dejection was not his health but his wife's estrangement from him following the death of their daughter Clara on September 24, 1818. Mary seems to have felt that her husband was indirectly responsible for the death of the child because he had insisted on making a hurried journey in hot weather to Venice at a time when little Clara was sick. The child died shortly after the Shelley family reached Venice.

Other causes undoubtedly contributed to Shelley's death-wish at Naples. His first wife, Harriet Westbrook, and Mary Shelley's half sister, Fanny Imlay, had committed suicide; the courts had taken from him the custody of his two children by Harriet; friends had turned against him; his poetry was neglected by the public and condemned by the critics, and he was plagued by financial and personal problems. Shelley experienced one of the lowest periods of his life while he was in Naples. His desire to free himself by death from his troubles does not necessarily reveal any moral or character weakness but an understandably profound discouragement at a time when everything seemed to be going wrong. Nature, no matter how beautiful, was of little help.

Questions and Essay Topics

1. Is Shelley yielding to self-pity in "Stanzas"?

2. Compare this dejection poem with dejection poems written by other romantic poets.

3. Is a poet necessarily unmanly in complaining about the hardships of his life and wishing it were over?

4. Are poems like "Stanzas" dispiriting to the reader? Explain.

5. Read the account of Shelley's stay in Naples in Newman Ivey White's biography of Shelley.

"Sonnet: England in 1819"

Summary

The king is dying, old, blind, insane, and despised. His sons are objects of public scorn. His ministers run the country for their own selfish interests. The people are hungry and oppressed. The army is used to destroy liberty and to collect booty. The law is manipulated to protect the rich and enchain the poor. Religion is in a state of apathy. Parliament denies Roman Catholics their civil rights. But out of this unhappy state of affairs may come a revolution that will right all wrongs.

Commentary

"Sonnet: England in 1819" is one of Shelley's most vigorous political statements. The language is unusually vivid and emphatic and shows how deeply Shelley's feelings were involved. The sonnet is probably the best of a group of political poems written by Shelley in 1819 which were inspired by Shelley's indignation in regard to the condition of England at that time. None of them were printed in 1819 because of publishers' fears of the strict libel laws. Any publisher who would print "Sonnet: England in 1819" ran the risk of being jailed or fined or both.

The king Shelley refers to in his poem is George III. In 1819, he was eighty-one years old, insane, blind, and deaf. He died the following year and was succeeded by George IV, the oldest of George III's dissolute sons, "mud from a muddy spring." His separation from his wife, Princess Caroline of Brunswick, after a year of marriage caused a public scandal, and his numerous affairs injured his reputation. English liberals, such as Shelley and Byron, regarded him with profound scorn both as prince regent (1811-20) and as king (1820-30). His cabinet ministers were arch-conservatives.

The "rulers who neither see, nor feel, nor know" are Lord Liverpool and his conservative cabinet. In calling them leeches who are bleeding their country, Shelley is indulging in hyperbole. They were men of integrity who happened to be in power at a time of general unrest caused by the unemployment and hunger that followed the end of the Napoleonic wars. There was rioting, some destruction of property, inevitable arrests and repressive measures. The cabinet suspended the Habeas Corpus act and passed laws severely limiting public gatherings. Shelley was convinced that revolution was going to break out in England, "a glorious Phantom" that would "illumine our tempestuous day."

The line "a people starved and stabbed in the untilled field" may be an allusion to the Peterloo massacre. On August 16, 1819, a large number of people in favor of parliamentary reform had gathered in St. Peter's Field in Manchester to hear a speech by Henry Hunt, a reformer. When troops made an attempt to arrest Hunt, a panic ensued in which eleven people were killed and four hundred were injured.

The army, "which liberticide and prey/ Makes as a two-edged sword to all who wield" it, seems to be a reference to the use of troops by the government to quell disturbances and repress liberty. "Golden and sanguine laws which tempt and slay" are laws that vested interests caused to be passed and which led to bloodshed. "Religion Christless, Godless" refers to the torpid state of the Anglican Church, from which it was aroused by the Oxford Movement in 1833. "Time's worst statute" refers to the restrictions under which English Roman Catholics were forced to live. They were not allowed to vote or sit in Parliament, preside over law courts, or enter the universities. "Catholic emancipation" had been a lively political issue for several years, and not until 1829 did Catholics recover most of their civil liberties.

Questions and Essay Topics

1. Shelley's sonnets "Ozymandias" and "England in 1819" are among Shelley's most forceful poems. Is there anything about the sonnet form that might account for this fact?

2. Read an account of the state of England following the Napoleonic wars. Was there real danger of a revolution in England?

3. Is Shelley lacking in charity and justice in describing George III as he does?

4. Does the main interest of the poem lie in its account of the condition of England in 1819? Is it also a work of art and therefore of permanent interest?

5. Does Shelley use figurative language in "Sonnet: England in 1819"?

"Ode to the West Wind"

Summary

The autumnal west wind sweeps along the leaves and "wingèd seeds." The seeds will remain dormant until spring. The wind is thus a destroyer and a preserver. The west wind also sweeps along storm clouds. It is the death song of the year. With the night that closes the year will come rain, lightning, and hail; there will be storms in the Mediterranean and the Atlantic. The poet pleads with the west wind to endow him with some of its power, for he feels depressed and helpless. If he were possessed of some of the power of the west wind, he would be inspired to write poetry which the world would read and by which it would be spiritually renewed, just as the renewal which is spring succeeds the dormancy of winter.

Commentary

Shelley appended a note to the "Ode to the West Wind" when it appeared in the *Prometheus Unbound* volume in 1820: "This poem was conceived and chiefly written in a wood that skirts the Arno, near Florence, and on a day when that tempestuous wind, whose temperature is at once mild and animating, was collecting the vapours which pour down the autumnal rains. They began, as I foresaw, at sunset with a violent tempest of hail and rain, attended by that magnificent thunder and lightning peculiar to the Cisalpine regions."

The note is interesting in that it shows that the poem came out of a specific experience. The imagery of the poem suggests a natural phenomenon that is observed while it is taking place. The fact that it was written near Florence, Dante's city, may explain why Shelley used *terza rima*, the stanza of Dante's *Divine Comedy*, but rare in English poetry, in the ode. *Terza rima* is a series of triplets with interlocking rhymes, aba, bcb, cdc, etc. Shelley modified the pattern by ending each of the five sections of the poem with a climactic couplet. In keeping with his *terza rima* stanza, he concentrates on the effects of the west wind on three classes of objects: leaves, clouds, and water. The combination of *terza rima* and the threefold effect of the west wind gives the poem a pleasing structural symmetry.

In the ode, Shelley, as in "To a Skylark" and "The Cloud," uses the poetic technique of myth, with which he had been working on a large scale in *Prometheus Unbound* in 1818. The west wind is a spirit, as is the skylark. It possesses great powers and for this very reason Shelley can pray to it for what he feels he is deeply in need of. He falls "upon the thorns of life," he bleeds; a "heavy weight of hours has chained and bowed" him. It was Shelley's belief that poetry, by appealing to the imagination, could stir the reader to action in a given direction. With Shelley, this direction was liberty and democracy. In *Prometheus Unbound*, he sketched the wonderful world of freedom that he dreamed of; readers, fascinated by Shelley's glowing descriptions, would be stimulated to want such a world too.

Unfortunately, readers seemed uninterested in his poetry, and democracy was not making progress in the Europe of 1819, when he wrote the poem. Shelley was profoundly discouraged, chained and bowed by a "heavy weight of hours." If he had the power possessed by his west wind's mythical divinity, readers would listen and freedom would prosper. "Be thou, Spirit fierce,/ My spirit! Be thou me, impetuous one! . . . Scatter . . . my words among mankind!/ Be through my lips to unawakened earth/ The trumpet of a prophecy!" By using the poetic device of myth, Shelley is able to indulge in wish-thinking without seeming to and, at the same time, he can strengthen the virtue of hope in himself. The poem ends optimistically: "O Wind,/ If Winter comes, can Spring be far behind?" Freedom will grow, no matter what obstacles there may be, and Shelley's words will help it grow.

Shelley's "Ode to the West Wind" is a good example of Shelley's poetic mind at work, and when it is at work, it is heaping up similes and metaphors. It is Shelley's extravagant fondness for metaphorical language that makes him all too often obscure and his subject matter thin. He is prone to be swept away by words, to be mastered by them, rather than to be a master of them. The leaves are driven from the presence of his west wind divinity "like ghosts from an enchanter fleeing." The simile is not based in reality nor is it functional. No doubt it comes from Shelley's early reading, much of which consisted of pulp fiction that dealt in enchanters, demons, and all forms of the supernatural moving about in an atmosphere of horror. The wind then changes from an enchanter to a carter driving a load of wingèd seeds to "their dark wintry bed" where they will lie like corpses in their graves until they are summoned to arise by the trumpet of the spring wind. The spring wind drives sweet buds "like flocks to feed in air" just as the west wind drives the leaves. The buds are not left as buds; they are transformed into sheep.

In the second stanza, the clouds are at once leaves "shook from the tangled boughs of Heaven and Ocean" and they are also "angels of rain and lightning." They are also, apparently, the "locks of the approaching storm," and they remind the poet of the locks on the head of "some fierce Maenad." The west wind is both a stream and a funeral song, and the coming night will be a huge tomb built by rain clouds carried by the wind.

In the third stanza, the west wind is the awakener of the Mediterranean Sea, lulled to sleep by its own currents and seeing in its sleep "old palaces and towers . . . overgrown with azure moss and flowers." The effect of the west wind on the Atlantic is to cut it into chasms as with a huge-bladed weapon and to inspire fear in the seaweed growing on the bottom. The contrast between the simplicity of the language in stanzas four and five, where Shelley is talking about himself, is the difference between dense jungle and treeless plain. When Shelley describes, the metaphors fall so thick and fast that the reader should perhaps simply yield without resistance to the incantation of the language. Shelley sometimes succeeds by sheer accumulation of language. Critics have noted Shelley's hypnotic power. The breathless sweep of accumulated language may perhaps be felt justifiable by the reader in a poem on a violent wind. Something which has the power of the wind is conveyed by the sheer mass of mellifluous, figurative language of the first three stanzas.

Questions and Essay Topics

1. Do you think that Shelley uses too much figurative language in the "Ode to the West Wind"?

2. What makes an ode different from any other type of lyric?

3. Is Shelley indulging in self-pity in the "Ode"?

4. Is Shelley's west wind in reality both a destroyer and a preserver?

5. Is the simile of seeds lying like corpses in their graves a good one?

"The Cloud"

Summary

The cloud brings rain, moisture, hail, and snow, and gives shade. It is infused with electricity which acts as its guide in the form of lightning accompanied by thunder. When the cloud covers the rising sun, it causes its beams to be spread out over the sky. At evening the cloud floats over the setting sun like a bird; at night, the cloud provides a thin covering for the moon. Where the cloud cover is removed by the wind, the moon and stars are reflected in the earth's bodies of water.

The cloud under certain conditions forms a ring around the sun and the moon. During storms the cloud spreads across the sky like a roof. At other times the rainbow acts as an arch of triumph for the cloud to march under. The cloud, formed in the sky, draws its substance from the earth and water below it and is part of a never-ending cycle in which it alternately disappears and reappears.

Commentary

In "The Cloud," Shelley is again the myth-maker. The cloud is not merely a physical substance but seems to be an immortal minor divinity (such as a naiad or a Nereid, which in classical mythology were associated with water). By employing this form of personification, Shelley is able to endow nature with the powers and attributes of immortals. Thus his cloud is not only capable of changing its form almost at will but is incapable of dying as well: "I change, but I cannot die."

Shelley's cloud is almost bewilderingly multiform. It begins as a gardener watering flowers, changes to a mother or nurse shading a child from the midday sun while the child takes a nap, becomes a bird that shakes dew from its wings to awaken the buds (which are babies rocked to rest on the breast of their mother the earth), and becomes a thresher wielding a flail. It laughs, sifts, sleeps, folds its wings like a bird, puts a girdle around the sun, becomes a roof, marches through a triumphal arch, is a baby daughter, passes "through the pores of the ocean and shores," and tears down an empty tomb. As a divinity, it can be and do a multiplicity of things. Shelley's "The Cloud" is compact with images, which, taken together, give the reader a good account of this natural phenomenon in the language of poetry.

Shelley's "Cloud," although extraordinarily rich in changing imagery, presents no special difficulty except perhaps in the second stanza, in which he makes lightning the pilot of the cloud. What Shelley is saying is that atmospheric electricity or lightning is formed in the tiny droplets of vapor that make up the clouds. He is merely asserting a familiar fact.

In addition to making lightning the guide of the cloud, Shelley subordinates the lightning to some force in the earth which attracts it. He has his cloud say:

> Over earth and ocean, with gentle motion,
> This pilot is guiding me,
> Lured by the love of the genii that move
> In the depths of the purple sea;
> Over the rills, and the crags, and the hills,
> Over the lakes and the plains,
> Wherever he dream, under mountain or stream,
> The Spirit he loves remains.

Shelley's genii are Moslem spirits that inhabit the earth and exercise supernatural power. Erasmus Darwin, an eighteenth-century poet-scientist, had used the word metaphorically in his *Botanic Garden,* where Shelley probably found it. The Spirit whom the lightning loves seems to be the genii in a singular form, but Shelley is not very clear here. He may have changed from the plural to the singular for the sake of a needed rime: *remains.* The genii are probably meant to poetically present the theory of atmospheric electricity, drawn by the sun from the earth as water vapor, returning to the earth as lightning, dew, frost, and rain. Shelley's genii therefore represents the phenomenon that when an electrically charged cloud approaches the earth's surface, an opposite charge is induced in the earth's surface. When there exists sufficient electrical potential, a lightning flash occurs. Shelley's knowledge of atmospheric electricity, although expressed in highly figurative language, is nevertheless accurate.

Questions and Essay Topics

1. Is there any reason to believe that Shelley's "The Cloud" is a symbolic poem; that is, not really about clouds but about something else?

2. Is "The Cloud" in any way a confessional poem about Shelley himself?

3. Is there too much imagery in "The Cloud"?

4. Is the imagery always accurate, functional, and effective?

5. Do the rimes occur too frequently in "The Cloud"?

"To a Skylark"

Summary

A skylark soars into the sky singing happily. As it flies upward, the clouds of evening make it invisible, but its song enables the poet to follow its flight. All the earth and air is filled with its song. The unseen but still singing skylark is compared to a poet composing, a maiden in love, a glowworm throwing out its beams of light, a rose in bloom diffusing its scent, and the sound of rain on twinkling grass. Songs sung in praise of love or wine or music played for a wedding or a celebration cannot compare in loveliness with the song of the skylark.

What accounts for the happiness of the song of the skylark? It is free from all that gives pain to man. It knows what lies beyond death and has no fear. Even if man freed himself from hate, pride, and fear, man's joy would not equal the skylark's. The secret of its capacity to sing so happily would be an incomparable gift for the poet. If the skylark could communicate to Shelley half its happiness, then he would write poetry that the world would read as joyfully as he is listening to the song of the bird.

Commentary

Mary Shelley wrote about "The Skylark": "In the Spring we spent a week or two near Leghorn. . . . It was on a beautiful summer evening while wandering among the lanes whose myrtle hedges were the bowers of the fire-flies, that we heard the carolling of the skylark." Like the "Ode to the West Wind," "The Skylark" was inspired by a specific experience, but Shelley's interest in the skylark is not that of the bird lover or the bird watcher. What he is fascinated by is the happiness that, for him, is present in the song of the bird. He doesn't say that he sees the bird, but it would seem that he has watched it leave the ground and disappear into the bright clouds above the setting sun, for he says that "the pale purple even/ Melts around thy flight." The color of the bird, its flight pattern, the quality of sound which distinguishes its song from that of other birds — in short, the individuality of the bird — the reader learns nothing about from reading "To a Skylark." Shelley has converted the bird or, specifically, the bird's song into a symbol of happiness. The poem, then, is not so much about a skylark as it is about happiness. The singing bird is personified as a "blithe" or happy spirit in the first line of the poem.

Shelley pursues two main lines of thought in the poem. The first is an effort to determine to his own satisfaction with what the singing bird is comparable. This is a relatively unimportant matter. The reader merely learns what the singing skylark brings to Shelley's mind in the way of similes. The birdsong is like a poet composing, a maiden making music, a glowworm scattering light, and a rose diffusing its perfume. The similes have in common the fact that all four are, like the now unseen skylark, out of sight or not easily seen.

The second line of thought is central to the poem. What, Shelley asks, is the secret that accounts for the skylark's happiness, manifested in its song?

> What objects are the fountains
>   Of thy happy strain?
> What fields, or waves, or mountains?
>   What shapes of sky or plain?
> What love of thine own kind? what ignorance of pain?

These questions lead him to an analysis of the human condition. Man knows pain, experiences weariness, annoyance, and love's satiety. He is plagued by hate and pride and fear. He cannot escape his past, thoughts of the future cause him worry, he longs for what does not exist, and his laughter is mixed with sorrow. He dreads death. The skylark, on the other hand, Shelley fancies, "of death must deem/ Things more true and deep/ Than we mortals dream." Therefore the skylark has no fear of death.

Shelley, in personifying the skylark, has created a myth, just as in "Ode to the West Wind" and "The Cloud." He has endowed his skylark with mind ("Teach us, Sprite or Bird,/ What sweet thoughts are thine"). The skylark is happy because it knows only what makes it happy. It has a decided advantage over human beings, who know both what makes them happy and what makes them unhappy. They fear death because they are ignorant of what lies beyond death, among other reasons. The skylark knows what lies beyond death, and the nature of what it knows banishes its fear of death. It is no wonder that it is incomparably happy.

Shelley knows that his skylark is merely a bird with a song that, to the human ear, sounds like a happy song. He is indulging in fancy and has no intention whatever of deceiving the reader or himself. The exquisite happiness that his ear has heard in the song of the nightingale has carried him away. In the last stanza of the poem he appeals to the creature of his imagination to teach him half the gladness "that thy brain must know." Happiness is the secret of the lovely song of the skylark; if Shelley possessed only half of the "gladness" of the skylark, he could write poetry that the world would read with the same rapt attention he is giving to the song of the skylark that his ears hear.

Questions and Essay Topics

1. "To a Skylark" has been criticized as a structurally loose poem; it has been said that the order of some of the stanzas could be changed without making any essential change in the poem. Is the criticism a just and valid one?

2. Shelley, in the first two lines of the poem, denies that the skylark is really a skylark: "Bird thou never wert." Later he admits that the skylark may really be a bird after all: "Teach us, Sprite or Bird,/ What sweet thoughts are thine." Is the admission to be considered a weakness in the poem?

3. Is elevating the skylark to the rank of spirit a weakness in the poem?

4. Is "Ode to the West Wind" a better poem than "To a Skylark" in the arrangement of its parts?

5. If Shelley shared half the happiness he feels the skylark possesses, readers would read his poems with greater attention. Do you think he refers to the poems he has written or to the poems he would write? If the latter, what might their subject matter be?

"To Night"

Summary

Shelley calls on night to come quickly: "Swiftly walk o'er the western wave,/ Spirit of Night." All day long he has waited for night; day has lingered like an unwanted guest. Neither death nor sleep will serve as a substitute. Death will come too soon in any case and sleep will come when night is over. Neither can give what night can give.

Commentary

As in "Ode to the West Wind," "The Cloud," and "To a Skylark," Shelley uses myth-making as his device for apostrophizing night. This device enables him to give life and personality to a natural phenomenon.

The poem was written in 1821, a year before Shelley's death. Like other lyrics of Shelley's last years, it reflects depression and a kind of weary resignation. It is not a cheerful poem, but, on the other hand, it does not incorporate a death wish like his "Stanzas Written in Dejection" of December, 1818. Shelley explicitly rejects death in the poem. Yet the poem has a touch of morbidity in it: night is preferred to day, and it is not invoked so that with it will come sleep. Shelley wants to escape from day and seek refuge in night, but in the poem he doesn't tell us why he wants night to come.

The *raison d'être* of this strange little poem probably lies in Shelley's personality and in his state of mind when he wrote the poem. People found Shelley friendly and sociable, but he preferred the company of books and his own thoughts to society. During the day, he found it impossible to avoid the company of others; there was no escaping the many demands on his time and energy. At night, when others were sleeping, Shelley could withdraw into his own private world to read and meditate as he pleased. Night brought rest and peace, freedom from society and the everyday demands of life, and also the opportunity to indulge in the dark thoughts that the frequently unsatisfactory circumstances of his life made inevitable. One of these unsatisfactory circumstances in 1821 was that he had become infatuated with a young Italian girl, Emilia Viviani. His wife, Mary, was by this time well acquainted with Shelley's propensity to be strongly attracted to young women in whom he felt he detected certain affinities to be found nowhere else, and she had learned to be tolerant. But inevitably tensions developed, for Mary realized that she could not be everything for Shelley that he required. In September of 1821, Emilia married, and Shelley, who had idealized her in his "Epipsychidion," was cut off from all further communication with her. Her marriage left him, as he wrote to his friend John Gisborne, "in a sort of morbid quietness." The Emilia episode was the major source of emotional tumult in Shelley's life in 1821.

"To Night" is so personal a poem that it is unlikely that it owes anything to poems with a night setting such as Milton's "Il Penseroso" nor to the eighteenth-century "Graveyard School of Poetry," which preferred night to day as a time for serious meditation. "To Night" is probably to be linked with other poems written in 1821, such as the moving "A Lament":

> O World! O life! O time!
> On whose last steps I climb,
>   Trembling at that where I had stood before;
> When will return the glory of your prime?
>   No more—Oh, never more!
>
> Out of the day and night
> A joy has taken flight:
>   Fresh spring, and summer, and winter hoar,
> Move my faint heart with grief, but with delight
>   No more—Oh, never more!

Questions and Essay Topics

1. Is it to be regarded as a defect in "To Night" that Shelley doesn't tell his readers why he is waiting for night to come?

2. In line 11, Shelley makes *day* feminine; in line 19, masculine. How is this inconsistency to be accounted for?

3. Why is death called the brother of night?

4. Do you think that Shelley is referring to one particular night or night in general in the poem?

5. Does the poem contain any hint of the "boon" he asks of night?

6. Investigate the theme of night in late eighteenth-century poetry.

Adonais

Summary

The poet weeps for Keats who is dead and who will be long mourned. He calls on Urania to mourn for Keats who died in Rome (sts. I-VII). The poet summons the subject matter of Keats' poetry to weep for him. It comes and mourns at his bidding (sts. VIII-XV). Nature, celebrated by Keats in his poetry, mourns him. Spring, which brings nature to new life, cannot restore him (sts. XVI-XXI). Urania rises, goes to Keats' death chamber and laments that she cannot join him in death (sts. XXII-XXIX). Fellow poets mourn the death of Keats: Byron, Thomas Moore, Shelley, and Leigh Hunt (sts. XXX-XXXV). The anonymous *Quarterly Review* critic is blamed for Keats' death and chastized (sts. XXXVI-XXXVII).

The poet now urges his readers not to weep any longer. Keats has become a portion of the eternal and is free from the attacks of reviewers. He is not dead; it is the living who are dead. He has gone where "envy and calumny and hate and pain" cannot reach him. He is "made one with Nature." His being has been withdrawn into the one Spirit which is responsible for all beauty. In eternity other poets, among them Chatterton, Sidney, and Lucan, come to greet him (sts. XXXVIII-XLVI). Let anyone who still mourns Keats send his "spirit's light" beyond space and be filled with hope, or let him go to Rome where Keats is buried. Let him "Seek shelter in the shadow of the tomb./ What Adonais is, why fear we to become?" He is with the unchanging Spirit, Intellectual Beauty, or Love in heaven. By comparison with the clear light of eternity, life is a stain (sts. XLVII-LII).

The poet tells himself he should now depart from life, which has nothing left to offer. The One, which is Light, Beauty, Benediction, and Love, now shines on him. He feels carried "darkly, fearfully, afar" to where the soul of Keats glows like a star, in the dwelling where those who will live forever are (sts. LIII-LV).

Commentary

Shelley did not hear of the death of Keats in Rome, in February, 1821, until some weeks later. The relations between the two were not close. They had met and there had been a few letters exchanged. Shelley had shown sympathy when he learned of Keats' intention to go to Italy for his health and had invited him to be his guest. Shelley also knew of the attacks of the reviewers on Keats' poetry. His own poetry had fared no better than Keats' at the hands of the Tory reviewers. When the report of Keats' death reached him, he was convinced that Keats had been hounded to death by the reviewers, so he decided to write a defense of Keats and an attack on the Tory reviewers. The result was *Adonais,* which he wrote in the spring and published in the fall of 1821. To make doubly clear his aggressive intention in the poem, he provided it with a preface in which he called the Tory reviewers "wretched men" and "literary prostitutes." The reviewer of Keats' *Endymion* in the *Quarterly* was accused of murder. *Adonais* and its preface brought down on Shelley the wrath of the conservative reviewers. *Blackwood's Magazine* attacked him with special savagery. The reception of *Adonais* deepened Shelley's despairing conviction that he had failed as a poet. He wrote on January 25, 1822, to Leigh Hunt: "My faculties are shaken to atoms. . . . I can write nothing; and if *Adonais* had no success, and excited no interest what incentive can I have to write?"

Shelley gave his elegy a title that pointed clearly to his intention to attack the reviewers. Adonis in classical mythology was killed by a boar; Adonais (a variant of Adonis coined by Shelley) was killed by reviewers. It was in the tradition of elegy to use proper names taken from classical literature. Shelley's coinage may have been intended to forestall the misapprehension that the poem was about Adonis. Adonais was close enough to serve his purpose. For his stanza he picked the Spenserian, which was perhaps unfortunate. The long nine-line Spenserian can be a kind of bushel basket to poets inclined to wordiness, as Shelley was.

For his primary models in writing a formal elegy, Shelley went to two Sicilian Greek poets, Bion and Moschus. He had translated part of Bion's "Lament for Adonis" and Moschus' "Lament for Bion." His borrowings from them are very extensive and constitute the weakest part of his elegy, namely, the first half, which is full of personifications that are given speaking and acting roles. His indebtedness to Moschus is particularly great. In Moschus, groves and gardens, nymphs, Echo, the Loves, towns and cities, the muse, and pastoral poets mourn for Bion. When Bion died, trees dropped their fruit and blossoms faded, according to Moschus. In Bion's "Lament," Shelley found the death of Adonis from the attack of a boar, the description of the corpse in death, the thorns tearing the feet of Venus as she walked, the Loves cutting off their curls to cast on Adonis, washing his wound and fanning his body, and a good deal more that is also in Moschus.

The poem begins with a confident assertion that the fame of Keats will live forever. Shelley then addresses five stanzas to the muse Urania which do little to advance the movement of the poem and which furnish a critical estimate of Keats that posterity has not supported. Shelley felt that Keats was a promising poet, not a poet who had achieved greatness. Stanzas IX through XIV are devoted to the thoughts and feelings which went into Keats' poetry; they are very swollen with personification and metaphor and are probably the least interesting part of the poem. Stanzas XV, XVI, and XVII likewise contribute little to the elegy. *Adonais* becomes interesting when Shelley, following the lead of Moschus, mediates on the return of spring in all its freshness and sadly contrasts it with the finality of death, from which there is no return: "Alas! that all we loved of him should be,/ But for our grief, as if it had not been,/ And grief itself be mortal." Stanzas XVIII through XXI move the reader by appealing to common experience.

Stanzas XXII-XXXV are devoted to what in elegy is sometimes called the "procession of mourners." Urania, properly the muse of astronomy but who had been made the heavenly muse of lofty poetry in *Paradise Lost* by Milton, is first in the procession. The most interesting part of this overlong section of the poem assigned to Urania is her attack on the Tory reviewers who are called "herded wolves," "obscene ravens," and "vultures" by Shelley. The human mourners, Byron, Thomas Moore, Shelley himself, and Keats' friend Leigh Hunt follow Urania. Shelley's self-portrait in stanzas XXXI-XXXIV, besides being overlong, is marred by the self-pity which is the common denominator in all his poetic self-portraits. Of the four poets included, only Hunt can be considered an admirer of Keats' poetry. Shelley liked Keats' unfinished "Hyperion" but not much else by Keats. Byron didn't like it and Moore was apparently not familiar with it. Other prominent living poets such as Wordsworth, Coleridge, Scott, and Robert Southey, the poet laureate, are not included in the "procession" probably because they were Tories. Since Keats was not well-known as a poet in his lifetime, Shelley faced a practical difficulty in forming a procession.

In stanzas XXXVI and XXXVII Shelley turns to the anonymous reviewer of Keats' *Endymion* in the *Quarterly Review* (now known to be John Wilson Croker) and calls him a "nameless worm," a "noteless blot," a snake, and a beaten hound. His punishment will be remorse, self-contempt, and shame. With the attack on the *Quarterly* reviewer, the mourning section of the poem ends and the consolation section begins (XXXVIII). Keats has been released from the burden of life: "He has outsoared the shadow of our night;/ Envy and calumny and hate and pain,/ . . . Can touch him not and torture not again. . . . He is made one with Nature." He has been absorbed into Shelley's rather elusive deity, the nature and function of which we can derive only from his poetry. The deity which Shelley variously calls a Power, the one Spirit, and the One is responsible for all the beauty in the world. It "wields the world with never-wearied love,/ Sustains it from beneath, and kindles it above." Keats, who created beauty by his poetry, will continue to create beauty as part of the one Spirit. Shelley's god is not a personal god but a force, and Keats will not retain his personal identity in the hereafter as part of this force. In stanzas XLV and XLVI, he classes Keats with those poets who died too young to achieve the full maturity of such poets as Thomas Chatterton, Sir Philip Sidney, and the Roman poet Lucan.

Stanzas XLVII-LII form a unit addressed to the person who still mourns Keats in spite of Shelley's exhortation to bring mourning to an end. In stanza XLVII, a difficult stanza, such a person is invited to reach out imaginatively in spirit beyond space. Then he will see existence in true perspective and be filled with hope. He will see the true relation between life and death and realize that life constricts and death releases. In stanzas XLVIII-LI, the mourner is invited to go to Rome where Keats is buried. There "in the shadow of the tomb," in beautiful surroundings (in the preface to *Adonais*, Shelley says of the cemetery where Keats is buried that "it might make one in love with death, to think that one should be buried in so sweet a place."), he will remember what Keats has become and will lose his reason to mourn. Keats is with the One, unchanging ultimate reality. To be with the One is to be in "the white radiance of Eternity," by comparison with which life is a stain. Death is a release into Eternity.

In the last three stanzas of the poem, Shelley turns to himself. He asks himself why he should want to cling to life any longer. His hopes are gone, "a light is passed from the revolving year,/ And man, and woman; and what still is dear/ Attracts to crush, repels to make thee wither." This is one of Shelley's many despairing confessions of his unhappiness and one of his most explicit death wishes. Shelley's desire to be absorbed into the One Spirit, to join Keats seems motivated more by despair than by ardent desire to be with his deity, which is called Light, Beauty, and Benediction. Shelley's impulsive nature gives the concluding stanza an intensity which is belied by the hatred of life revealed in stanza LIII.

Shelley's most famous poem suffers by comparison with Milton's *Lycidas*, the standard by which English elegies will inevitably be judged. Shelley says much less than Milton in many more words, and the most eloquent parts of *Adonais* are not equal to the most eloquent parts of *Lycidas*. Shelley is merely prolix where Milton is meaningful. A close examination of *Adonais* shows that rhyme frequently determined his choice of words. *Adonais* does not have a firm structure; its development seems haphazard. The image of Keats given by Shelley is that of a weakling killed by reviewers. The biography of Keats reveals a quite different Keats—a manly, slightly belligerent poet not apt to be profoundly discouraged by harsh criticism. (In the preface to *Adonais*, Shelley remarks that "the poor fellow seems to have been hooted from the stage of life. . . .") The heaven in which Shelley places Keats is not Christian; it is not Milton's heaven where "tears are wiped forever from [our] eyes." Shelley's consolation section could hardly have been very consoling to Keats' relatives and friends. *Adonais* is, however, an often forceful and certainly generous defense of an insufficiently appreciated brother poet.

Questions and Essay Topics

1. Read Bion's "Lament for Adonis" and Moschus' "Lament for Bion" and compare them with *Adonais*.

2. Compare and contrast Milton's *Lycidas* and Shelley's *Adonais*.

3. Draw up a set of standards for an ideal elegy and apply them to *Adonais*.

4. Can *Adonais* be considered a pastoral elegy?

5. What parts of *Adonais* can be called digressions? Can the presence of these digressions be defended successfully?

6. Compare Shelley's deity in "Hymn to Intellectual Beauty" with his deity in *Adonais*.

7. Look up the myth of Venus and Adonis and determine how much of it Shelley has embodied in *Adonais*.

8. Make a comparative reading of the chapters on *Adonais* in Carlos Baker's *Shelley's Major Poetry*, Edward B. Hungerford's *Shores of Darkness*, James A. Notopoulos' *The Platonism of Shelley*, and Earl R. Wasserman's *The Subtler Language*.

SELECTED BIBLIOGRAPHY

Biography

WHITE, NEWMAN IVEY. *Shelley.* 2 vols. New York: Alfred A. Knopf, 1940. Standard biography. Analyses of many poems.

Editions

HUTCHINSON, THOMAS, ed. *The Complete Poetical Works of Shelley.* Oxford: Clarendon Press, 1904. Best one-volume edition of Shelley's poems.

INGPEN, ROGER, and WALTER E. PECK, eds. *The Complete Works of Percy Bysshe Shelley.* 10 vols. London: Ernest Benn, 1926-30. Standard but no longer complete edition of Shelley's works.

Reference and Criticism

BAKER, CARLOS. *Shelley's Major Poetry: The Fabric of a Vision.* Princeton: Princeton University Press, 1948. A study of the longer poems.

BLOOM, HAROLD. *Shelley's Mythmaking.* New Haven: Yale University Press, 1959.

BUTTER, PETER. *Shelley's Idols of the Cave.* Edinburgh: University Press, 1954.

REIMAN, DONALD H. *Percy Bysshe Shelley.* New York: Twayne Publishers, 1969. A very useful Shelley handbook. Contains synopses and analyses of all of Shelley's longer poems and some of the shorter ones.

REITER, SEYMOUR. *A Study of Shelley's Poetry.* Albuquerque: University of New Mexico Press, 1967. A study of thirty-one of Shelley's poems in chronological order. The best book on Shelley's poetry.

WASSERMAN, EARL R. *The Subtler Language: Critical Readings of Neo-classic and Romantic Poems.* Baltimore: Johns Hopkins University Press, 1959. Contains readings of Shelley's "Mont Blanc," "The Sensitive Plant," and *Adonais*.

NOTES

NOTES

NOTES

NOTES

NOTES